to My Sister 1 Hill
family

wt!

PETTICOATS, POLITICS, AND PIROUETTES

Oklahoma Women from 1900-1950

Glenda Carlile

Glenda Carlile [signature]

NEW "," FORUMS

Stillwater, Oklahoma
U.S.A.

NEW FORUMS PRESS INC.

Published in the United States of America
by New Forums Press, Inc.
1018 S. Lewis St.
Stillwater, OK 74074
www.newforums.com

Library of Congress Cataloging-in-Publication Data
Pending

This book may be ordered in bulk quantities at dis-
count from New Forums Press, Inc., P.O. Box 876,
Stillwater, OK 74076 [Federal I.D. No. 73 1123239].
Printed in the United States of America.

International Standard Book Number: 1-58107-120-5

Edited by Carol Welsh.

Cover design by Mark Herndon.

First paperback edition / 1 2 3 4 5 6 7 8 9 0

Acknowledgements

It has been said that writing a book is a solitary experience. I have found this to be untrue. This book could not have been accomplished without the help, support, and encouragement from many others. One of my greatest pleasures has been working with so many wonderful people during the research, writing, and production of this book.

My heartfelt thanks to:

The women who made such outstanding contributions to their state and country and their families and friends who shared their pictures, scrapbooks, and memories.

Liz Codding and Sue Stees, friends and fellow writers who gave so generously their time, expertise, and encouragement in proofing the manuscript.

The staff of the Oklahoma Historical Society (especially Bill Welge, Rodger Harris, Judith Michener, and Chester Cowen), The Oklahoma Heritage Association, and the directors of the excellent museums across the state for help in research and providing photographs.

Molly Griffis of Levite of Apache Publishing Company and Ann Ogle, manager of the Oklahoma Historical Society Bookstore for technical advice; and the many historians, writers, and craftsmen who shared their knowledge.

Artist Mark Herndon, editor Carol Welsh, and typesetter and printer Tom Keneda for taking a manuscript and creating a book.

Joyce, Sandy, Gayle, Marilyn, Margo, Roma, and the many other friends who have given encouragement.

Most of all my love and sincere appreciation to my family who, while I was involved with this project, have had to share my time, sometimes begrudgingly but always with love – my husband, Tom; my parents, Glenn and Alda Horn; my children, Kim, Stacey, and Margaret; and my grandchildren, Jayson, Ryane, Cooper, Jackson, and Olivia, who provide inspiration and the promise for the future.

CONTENTS

FOREWORD

Oklahoma history is many things to many people. To some, it is Indian history, a diverse topic that rises in the pre-historic mist of tribal beginnings and continues with the rich tapestry of Indian culture today. To others, the most important theme is pioneer history, with the dramatic land openings and the courageous battles to survive and prosper in a new land.

Whether it is Indian history, pioneer history, military history, or even the more traditional political history, each topic shares a common thread that holds the entire saga of Oklahoma history together. That connecting tissue is the story of Oklahoma women, the topic of this new book by noted author, Glenda Carlile.

In these pages, the reader will sample the diversity of our shared history, from politics and business to art and high society, presented in a biographical format that is easy to read and dramatic enough to remember. At the same time, there is an important lesson that comes through the narrative description, and that is the importance of leadership. Whether it was fighting for civil rights or struggling to make a living, the will to make a difference, the determination to make their world a better place to live comes through in every biographical profile.

Yes, Oklahoma history is many things to many people, and every reader will find something to like in these pages.

Dr. Bob L. Blackburn, 1995
Deputy Director, Oklahoma Historical Society

PROLOGUE

Oklahomans have become familiar with the saying, "The Oklahoma Pioneer Spirit." It does not necessarily mean arriving in Oklahoma in a covered wagon or living in a sod house. Rather, the Oklahoma Pioneer Spirit conveys an image of faith, courage, resourcefulness, love, compassion, talent, and helpfulness. Nowhere is that Oklahoma Pioneer Spirit more visible than in its women.

Oklahomans in petticoats have excelled and have been recognized all over the world for their countless achievements. They have made outstanding contributions in the arts, politics, medicine, civil rights, and society in general. Without women there would not be a society, for they are the glue that holds together the families and the communities.

Buckskin, Calico, and Lace, Oklahoma's Territorial Women, described the courageous women who came to Oklahoma before statehood. Shortly after publication in 1990, work began on a sequel. The original title was to be *Oklahoma Women From Statehood to Space Age*. It quickly became apparent that there were far too many exciting and enterprising women to be included in one book covering almost one hundred years.

Thus the time period for *Petticoats, Politics, and Pirouettes* was shortened to a half century, from 1900 to 1950. Granted, many of the women may have been born before 1900, and their accomplishments may have continued long after 1950, but this is the period of their major achievements. Even with a shortened time frame, space prevented the inclusion of many women of noteworthy enterprises.

Oklahoma women have been virtually ignored by the historians. Some of this is understandable.

Oklahoma grew so quickly that some historians described the area as "Born Grown." There were enough conquests by the men to fill the history books. Women were so busy supporting these efforts and trying to civilize the new country, they did not have time to think that their efforts might have been extraordinary.

In the early days, women's worth was greatly underestimated. After all, women did not have the right to vote until 1918. Women themselves did not think their work was important. For instance, Alice Robertson, the first woman in the state and the second woman in the United States to be elected a member of the United States House of Representatives did not believe a woman should be in politics and voted against women's suffrage.

Oklahoma went through many rapid changes in the era of 1900 to 1950. An area that just a few years before had been open country of beautiful prairie with buffalo and Indians roaming the plains, rapidly changed to a state crisscrossed by railroads and dotted with oil rigs. During this time, Oklahoma became a state, sent soldiers to fight in two world wars, and went from periods of high economic growth to a great depression.

Oklahoma women not only participated in these events, they made valuable contributions. Although they wore petticoats these women were definitely not the weaker sex.

Augusta Metcalfe, a pioneer homesteader, worked in the fields, strung fence and branded cattle by daylight and at night painted the beautiful pictures of Oklahoma's landscape.

As Augusta preserved the history of Oklahoma with her paintbrush, Angie Debo recorded that history with a pen and paper. Their lives were similar in many ways; both arrived in Oklahoma by covered wagon and their own lives were studies of perseverance and success. Angie Debo's ambition was to be a college history teacher but after long years of preparation she found that field closed to women. Rather than giving up, she turned to writing Oklahoma history and is acknowledged as one of the best, if not the best, Oklahoma historians.

The Harvey girls rose early in the morning and went to bed late at night so that they could greet the passengers on the trains passing through the Territory. They were unafraid to go into areas sparsely populated to bring some sense of civilization and comfort to the people they served.

Oklahoma women rose to the top in the political field, not because they actively sought recognition but because of the acknowledgement of their qualifications and service. Alice Brown Davis became the first woman Chief of the Seminole Nation, because of her long years of service to her people. At sixty-five years of age, Alice Robertson became the first and only woman from Oklahoma to be elected to the United States House of Representatives. She was the second woman in the entire nation to be so honored and the first woman to ever preside over the United States House of Representatives.

Her mother, Ann Eliza Worcester Robertson was the first woman in the United States to receive a Ph.D. The honorary doctorate, in recognition of her linguistic studies, was from the University of Wooster, in Wooster, Ohio.

Perle Mesta not only achieved fame as the "Hostess with the Mostess" but also as one of the first women to represent the United States as an ambassador to a foreign country.

At the turn of the century, women began pursuing active careers in their own right. Whether married or single, many worked outside the home. Petticoats began appearing in professions where women had never dared to tread before. Dr. Theresa Hunt became the first woman dentist in Oklahoma. She was used to fighting for acceptance in a man's profession, and was surprised to find that Watonga accepted her for her skills, not her gender.

The oil boom days of the early 1920's influenced the lives of many Oklahoma women. Oil changed small communities into crowded boom towns over-night. The towns were full of adventurers and not all were men. Into the crowded, dirty oil towns came a vivacious spirited entertainer, Ruby Darby, known as the "Queen of the Oilfields."

Oil also made instant millionaires and a new way of life for the wealthy. Beautiful mansions, such as the Marland Mansion in Ponca City and Philbrook in Tulsa, were built. The wealthy spent lavishly on clothing, trips to Europe, private train cars and their own yachts. Jane Phillips was a good example of the wealthy socialite. Unlike some of the others, she still retained the values and friendships from her past. As a result, she was loved by her community and called "Aunt Jane."

Beauty was also much appreciated by the wealthy. Norma Smallwood, became the first Miss America from Oklahoma. She married the wealthy oilman Thomas Gilcrease.

Just as quickly as the oil brought wealth, the depression brought hardships. Oilman E. W. Marland lost his fortune and his wife, the beautiful Lyde Marland, never recovered from the shock. Her tragic life became one of Oklahoma's biggest mysteries.

"Terror in petticoats" became the nickname the FBI used in searching for one of the country's most wanted criminals. She was "Ma Barker" and she lived in Tulsa, Oklahoma.

The statement, "the world is a stage" certainly applied to Oklahoma dancers, who became famous appearing on stages all over the world. Oklahoma was privileged to have five world renowned ballerinas, who danced with the most famous ballet companies in the world. They were also all of Indian heritage. It was quite amazing to have five famous dancers from one state and for them all to be famous at approximately the same time.

As a child, Mignon Laird traveled across the country in a pullman railroad car that was also her father's medical clinic and the backdrop for their traveling med-opry show. She was famous before she could walk and rose to greater fame as a member of Zigfield Frolics.

Te Ata carried her stories of Indian Lore around the world and was declared the first Oklahoma State Treasurer. By the 1940's women were still pioneers. Rose Mary Hogan was a pioneer for women in the armed services. An army nurse, she was one of the first women to be held a prisoner of war during World War II. She was also one of the first women to receive the full rank of colonel.

Ada Lois Sipuel (Fisher) was a pioneer in the field of civil rights. A young black student at Langston University, she took her fight to be enrolled in the University of Oklahoma Law School all the way to the United States Supreme Court.

Every Oklahoma community has a Fern McFarland. Someone whose leadership capabilities and feisty personality make them the town leader. When combined with her great cooking and innovative marketing skills, it is easy to understand why "Granny Fern's Kitchen" became one of the most popular eating places in Oklahoma.

Oklahoma history has been recorded forever by Muriel Wright, the editor of the *Chronicles of Okla-*

homa from 1943 to 1973. Story-teller and author Alice Marriott recorded the stories and the culture of the Indians.

Petticoats, Politics and Pirouettes is a collection of stories of women from 1900 to 1950, and the amazing accomplishments they made to Oklahoma and to the entire world.

Pirouette is a term used in dancing to describe a rapid whirling upon the toes. This, of course describes many of the dancers in this book; the five Indian ballerinas, Ruby Darby and Mignon Laird.

The term is also symbolic of the great turns and movements forward, at a fast pace for women, from 1900 to 1950. This was a period of great changes for the entire country and a time of rapid acceleration for women. Oklahoma women rose to the challenge and pirouetted through the first half of the twentieth century with poise and promise.

They met the challenge of their time and are a beacon unto this day.

Anonymous

Dedicated to the memory of Pat Brock, my good friend for over thirty years, whose faith, courage, and dedication to family, friends, and profession was an inspiration to all who knew her.

Other books by author

Buckskin, Calico, and Lace
Oklahoma's Territorial Women

Co-authored with Liz Codding
Oklahoma Yesterday, Today, and Tomorrow
Calendars of historic and current events
Volume I - 1993
Volume II- 1994
Volume III- 1995

Augusta Metcalfe. Courtesy of Howard Metcalfe, Augusta's son.

AUGUSTA METCALFE

Oklahoma's Story Book Artist

Augusta Metcalfe's paintings always told a story, usually about life on the Oklahoma prairie. She homesteaded land in the Cheyenne-Arapaho Opening in 1893, ran a ranch and raised a child alone. Although her hands were rough from stringing fence and roping cattle, she was known for her fine detail and authentic and accurate paintings of Western life. She never had an art lesson, but is recognized as one of the great artists of the Southwest. Her paintings hang all over the world, recording Oklahoma's rich heritage, scenic beauty, and pioneer perseverance.

"Metcalfe!" As Howard Metcalfe moved to the front of the line to receive his mail, a cheer went up from the rest of his squadron. The Air Force Mechanic from Oklahoma waved to his buddies as he picked up his letter from home.

He glanced at the envelope. There was the familiar sketch of his pet deer beneath the return address. Howard knew better than to open the letter until he got back to the barracks. There, his buddies would be gathered around for their favorite entertainment - a letter from Howard's mother.

Although Howard was older than the other men in his unit, the handsome Oklahoman, with the stories of growing up in western Oklahoma, was well liked, especially since the revelation of "the letters from Mother". To the lonely G.I.'s in the South Pacific, the next best thing to getting a letter from one's own family, was sharing Howard's letters from his mother.

Howard's letters were different! Each letter was

---

full of water color or pencil sketches telling a story of life back home. Everyone got a kick out of trying to figure out the word pictures and an afternoon of relief from the pressures of World War II.

But for Howard, those scenes of the farm or his pet deer usually left him feeling homesick. He would see past the pictures to his mother back on the homestead, her hands raw and calloused from working in the fields all day. He would see her grey head and lined face in the lamplight, drawing pictures to record what she had observed that day. He was a long way from that ranch in Oklahoma, but he was proud that his mother's paintings were beginning, at long last, to be recognized. Fame was coming to Augusta Metcalfe, who would become known as the "Sagebrush Artist of the West" and "Oklahoma's Grandma Moses."

With paintbrush in hand, Augusta recorded life in the early days as vividly and accurately as other historians have with pen and paper. She never had an art lesson but she painted life as she saw it, and she was a part of Oklahoma pioneer life since homesteading in No Man's Land in 1893.

Edward G. Corson, Augusta's father, was an adventurer. Living in Philadelphia, Pennsylvania, in the mid-1880's he heard of the opportunities for a young man in the west. His wife, at forty years of age, with three small children, and a good job teaching school was not so eager to begin a new life. But Edward's enthusiasm convinced her to become a pioneer.

The family first moved to Illinois, then to Kansas, where in 1881, a daughter, Augusta, was born. In 1886, the wanderlust hit Edward again and he moved his family to the Oklahoma Panhandle to an area known as No Man's Land.

Augusta first displayed her talent for drawing

on that long trip by covered wagon. Her mother gave her a pen and paper and told her to draw what she saw. Everyone was amazed at the five year old's remarkable likeness of a horse. Her mother recognized a talent in the young artist, and sent samples of her drawings to her brother, a college professor in California. Through the years, this uncle would encourage the young artist and send her art supplies and paper.

When the Cheyenne-Arapaho country was opened in 1893, the family moved near Cheyenne. Each parent homesteaded a quarter section of land, and when Augusta was old enough, she homesteaded the quarter section next to theirs. Around 1900, Edward built the rock house that so often appeared in Augusta's paintings. Augusta lived in the house until 1940.

Although Augusta never attended school, she received an excellent education from her schoolteacher mother who tutored her at home. She also received her best education from the outdoors that

Augusta's pen and ink drawings of the home her father built near Durham.

she loved so much. She enjoyed riding her horse and playing with her dog and then sketching them on paper. She learned to record the day's events and her surroundings by painting what she saw.

Augusta's father passed away February 4, 1903, leaving Augusta and her mother to run the two farms. It was difficult work for the heartiest pioneer, but the two women managed quite well. In the spring they plowed the land and sowed the crops, tended them in the summer, and harvested in the fall. They cared for the cows, chickens, and other livestock, strung fence, mowed, branded the cattle, and doctored the sick livestock. At the same time, they tended to "women's duties" of keeping house, washing, ironing, sweeping and canning.

In her leisure time, Augusta drew pictures and played the fiddle. The little house rang with music when Augusta sold a cow and bought her mother an organ. It was not all work. In many of her paintings, Augusta recorded the fun times of attending socials, church gatherings and weddings on the prairie.

At twenty-five years of age, Augusta fell in love with and married Jim Metcalfe. In her short marriage, nothing changed much. Augusta continued running the farm and the home, even before her husband deserted her, leaving her with a two year old son, Howard. Howard was the apple of his mother's and grandmother's eyes, following them around the farm, helping with chores, and eventually taking over many of the duties. His life was much like Augusta's as a child, lots of hard work but good times that left lasting memories - school and church events and a home filled with music and laughter.

Through all the masculine duties, Augusta never lost her femininity, gentleness or her desire to paint beautiful settings. Painting could only be done between chores or late at night by lamplight. Often, her hands were rough and swollen from barbed wire scratches but somehow, they held a brush steady enough to put fine detail into authentic and accurate paintings of western life.

Her paintings reflected her life - not the hardships, but the beauty of the landscape and the people and the animals around her. She began illustrating for some of the eastern educational magazines, as well as the *Farmer's Stockman*, and other area publications.

One of her most unusual paintings was on a grain of corn. There was a blue sky with a garden scene of a lady sitting in the shade of the trees, listening to the red horn of an Edison phonograph. This painting on a kernel of corn demonstrated the fine detail Augusta was capable of painting. The miniature was sent to Thomas A. Edison and her son Howard proudly displays the letter, dated April 23, 1912, from Edison thanking Augusta.

In later years, she painted a picture of General Douglas McArthur on a china plate, had it fired, and mailed it to him. In return, he sent her a large photo of himself, personally autographed.

By 1911 Augusta was receiving some recognition for her paintings. She won first prize in the Oklahoma State Fair in 1909 and 1910. At the Amarillo Tri-State Fair, her paintings won first place in 1948, 1951, and 1952. She also won first place in several county fairs. Her son has a box filled with her many ribbons. An article appeared in the *Oklahoma Farmer Stockman* telling of this amazing gentle woman. She also began to sell some of her works and often traded pictures for some needed household or farm item. She continued illustrating articles for the *Sportsman Review* and other publications including a book entitled *Hang Onto the Willows*.

Augusta's fame began to spread outside of Oklahoma. In fact, she became better known in other states before official recognition in her home state. In 1950, *Life Magazine* contained an article about the sixty-nine year old "Sage Brush Artist," and for the first time the art critics in Oklahoma took notice of what a natural treasure was here in the state. In 1960, a representative from the Grand Central Art Gallery in New York City came to visit Augusta in Durham and almost persuaded her to return with her for a showing. Augusta decided not to go but sent many of her paintings.

By this time, Howard had returned to the farm, bringing with him a bride from California. The two women got along beautifully and the three of them lived together for 26 years. They formed a musical group and traveled around the area entertaining. Helen played the piano and Howard and his mother played the fiddle and the mandolin. Augusta had for years fiddled for local dances.

Augusta had been painting all her life but it was not until her older years that true recognition was given. In the 1950s and '60s, people would travel from all over the country to Durham, Oklahoma, just to meet Oklahoma's Sagebrush Artist, view her work and visit with this amazing woman. At 97, she was recognized the world over for her oil paintings, water colors and pen sketches. Her paintings hung all over the world, in homes, banks, office buildings, and art galleries.

In November of 1968, she was inducted into the Oklahoma Hall of Fame. That same year a local television station aired a one hour documentary on her life.

Augusta died in 1971. In 1983 she was inducted into the National Cowgirl Hall of Fame in Hereford,

Texas where she was described as "a true child of the West."

The title "story book artist" fit Augusta very well as her paintings really did tell tales of early day Oklahoma life. She painted pictures of pioneers arriving in Oklahoma in covered wagons, of an outdoor wedding in the sandhills, of young people arriving at a dance in the snow, and many pictures of her beloved animals. The pictures, so vividly realistic, tell the stories of the land and the people of a day gone by. She said," I paint it as I see it," and through her eyes many others have seen the glory and beauty of Oklahoma.

Letter from Mother. Dear Son, this will not arrive in time for the holidays. I intended to get it off some time ago.

Mrs. Alice Brown Davis, Chief of the Seminoles. Courtesy of Archives and Manuscripts Division of the Oklahoma Historical Society.

ALICE BROWN DAVIS

Chief of Seminoles

Tribal Council Members sitting around the Council Room at Wewoka, the capitol of the Seminole Nation, shook their heads in disbelief. They had just heard the news that President Warren G. Harding had appointed Alice Brown Davis as Chief of the Seminole Nation. True, it was now 1922 and times were different from the old days when the Seminoles had chosen their own Chief, usually a distinguished warrior such as the great Osceola. Osceola had led their tribe in the fight to remain in the East before being forced to move to Indian Territory in 1842.

Much had changed in the last eighty years. Now the Seminoles, although the smallest, were considered the most peaceful and law- observing of the Five Civilized Tribes. They had prospered and adjusted well to modern times, especially in the last thirty years under the leadership of Chief John F. Brown, Jr., the brother of Alice Brown Davis. Now they felt bewildered and insulted that the President had chosen a woman to lead them as chief.

It was agreed that Mrs. Davis was well qualified, had served them well, and was loved and respected by both the Indian and the white people - but still - she was a woman! Never before had a woman held such an office in the Seminole Nation.

The old council house once again rang with the oratory of protest. Seminole warriors and the old men of the nation came from far and wide to protest. But it was too late. The decision had been made, and Alice Brown Davis was appointed the first woman Chief of the Seminoles, an office she was to fill with great honor to the Seminole Nation.

Growing up near Park Hill, in the Cherokee Nation, the carefree young Alice had no idea of the destiny before her.

Her favorite activity was to ride in the buggy with her father, Dr. John F. Brown, as he made house calls. As they rode along, he entertained the inquisitive Alice with stories of how he had met her mother and why they were living in the Cherokee Nation.

Dr. Brown was a white man of Scottish descent who had been educated at the University of Edinbourough. He was the Government physician for the Seminoles in Florida and he accompanied them on the removal to the West. Dr. Brown told Alice how terrible the trip had been. Many of the Indians were forced to leave their homes with only the clothes on their backs. Many had become sick and died along the way. He said that the removals of the Five Civilized Tribes to Indian Territory were so dreadful that they had become known as the "Trail of Tears."

Along the way, Dr. Brown had fallen in love with and married a beautiful young Indian maiden named Lucy Redbird, of the Tiger Clan. It was frowned upon for a member to marry outside the tribe, but Dr. Brown was determined to marry the young girl who had stolen his heart.

Upon their arrival in Indian Territory, they settled in Park Hill, near Tahlequah, the Cherokee capitol. There, Dr. Brown prospered as a doctor, and Alice was born on September 10, 1852.

Alice's carefree childhood was interrupted when the Civil War moved into Indian Territory. Her family moved to Ft. Gibson where Alice attended a school taught by Miss Carrie Bushyhead, sister of Cherokee Chief Dennis Bushyhead.

After the war, the family moved to Greenhead Prairie, Pottawatomie County, where they lived in the Government Agency building. Their closest neighbors were the Jesse Chisholm (of Chisholm Trail Fame) family. Alice became best friends with Jesse's daughter, Jennie, a friendship that would last all their lives.

During the summer of 1867, cholera broke out among the Seminoles, killing hundreds of people. Dr. Brown worked night and day, with Alice often accompanying him on his calls to the sick. Fatigue and the plague finally caught up to the old doctor, who had dedicated his life to the Seminoles. Alice was only fifteen when he died in 1868.

After their father's death, Alice's brother, John Brown, Jr., took charge of the family and moved them to Seminole County. There, he established the Sasakwa trading post, becoming quite wealthy and involved with the affairs of the Seminole Nation. He eventually became the Principal Chief, a position he held for over thirty years.

Alice attended school at the old Seminole Mission and worked for her brother at the trading post. She was working at Sasakwa when a handsome young white man came in to buy furs and pecans. He was George Davis, who worked for the F. B. Severs Store in Okmulgee. George was twenty-three years old and had come to Indian Territory from Leroy, Kansas. The young couple fell in love and were married by Creek Reverend Sam Checote in Okmulgee, on January 20, 1874. They lived for a time in Okmulgee, returning to the Seminole Nation in 1882, with George Davis establishing a trading post in the north part of the Seminole Nation which he called Arbeka. When the first post office was established at Arbeka in 1882, George became the postmaster.

Alice and George became the parents of eleven children; the youngest was only three years old when

George died. Alice continued to run Arbeka and the post office, while raising their four sons and seven daughters. She also became quite involved in the affairs of the Seminole Nation.

In 1903, Alice spent three months at Santa Rosalia, Chihuahua State, Mexico, on tribal matters. Back in Oklahoma, she was able to clear the title for the townsite of Okemah, and signed every deed that was issued for lots sold on the opening day of the Okemah townsite. In 1905, she went to Palm Beach, Florida, to act as interpreter for the United States Government, in a celebrated murder trial where John Ashley was being tried for murder of De Soto Tiger, a prominent Seminole Indian. Also, in 1905, Alice accompanied a party of delegates from her tribe to Mexico City where they attempted to gain information on a vast tract of land granted the Seminoles by the Mexican Government many years previous.

In 1909, Alice was sent as an emissary from the Seminole Nation to the Seminoles still living in the Florida Everglades. She lived with them for many months, preaching to them and endeavoring to interest them in the advantages of civilization.

Alice again traveled to Mexico in 1910, seeking to obtain information on land ceded to the Seminoles by Mexico in 1840. Alice became quite respected for her knowledge of languages, her intelligence, and her willingness to always come to the aid of her people. She served as the official interpreter in the courts when any of the Seminole required her help. She was also known as a Christian educator and served in Indian mission work of the Southern Baptist Church. Although women were not usually allowed to enter into governmental affairs, Alice Brown Davis was so well respected she was consulted in most matters of importance.

The land allotted to the Seminoles was considered poor for agricultural purposes - rocky on clay hillsides, rough, covered with blackjack, persimmon, hickory and scrub timber. However, in the early 1900s, this poor territory became one of the most valuable properties owned by any people of Oklahoma or the United States, when oil was discovered southeast of Wewoka in 1922. The great Seminole oil field, drilled on Indian land, mushroomed into a million-dollar-a-day production that quickly made many members of the Seminole Nation very wealthy. Disputes over land titles and royalties arose and lawsuits were filed daily. The Seminoles turned to Alice for advice. Oil companies, banks, businessmen and others seeking to own properties among the Indians also turned to Alice to assist them in negotiations.

Chief John Brown, Alice's brother, had resigned in 1916 when it was believed that tribal affairs had been concluded. Now it was apparent that an administrator of the tribe's business was needed. It was logical that Alice Brown Davis should be selected.

History was made on August 19, 1922, when Alice Brown Davis was inaugurated at Muskogee as the first woman chief of the Seminoles. The ceremony was very formal and elaborate, contrary to past ceremonies that were accompanied by the beat of tom-toms and dancing.

The United States district courthouse was filled to capacity with tribal leaders from all parts of the state gathered to bestow honor on the only chieftainess in Indian Territory. The audience arose as Mrs. Davis was escorted to her seat by Major Victor M. Locke, Jr., Superintendent of the Five Civilized Tribes. Standing before a banner emblazoned with the great seal of the Seminole Nation, the oath of office was administered by W. J. Farver, a Choctaw.

The courthouse erupted with applause as if the audience suddenly realized the full historical significance of the occasion. Miss Alice Robertson, America's only woman member of Congress, extended her congratulations and presented a huge bouquet of American Beauty roses with the remark that she desired to present "the queen of roses to the queen of the Seminoles."

Major Locke, a former chief of the Choctaws, remarked that Alice did not attain the chieftainship of the Seminoles through hereditary privileges, but was selected solely upon her ability and qualifications that long service on behalf of her people had made prominent.

Dr. Benjamin Weeks, president of Bacone Indian College, said in congratulating Alice, that her mental training and character were two of her outstanding features. Representatives from the Cherokee, Choctaw, Chickasaw, and Creek Nations congratulated Chief Davis and pledged their support.

Alice Brown Davis served her people as chief from 1922 until her death in 1935. In 1930, Alice was inducted into the Oklahoma Hall of Fame. In 1950, the Davis House at the University of Oklahoma was named in her honor. In 1961, she was selected for the American Indian Hall of Fame, and in 1964, a bronze bust of Alice Brown Davis was sculpted by Willard Stone and unveiled at the World's Fair in New York City.

Dr. THERESA HUNT TYLER

Watonga's First Dentist

Eight year old Theresa Hunt came through the back door into the kitchen, sailed her hat across the floor, and announced, "I know what I am going to do when I grow up. I am going to be a dentist."

Theresa had just returned from an appointment with the local dentist. She was impressed with the neatness and cleanliness of the office, the friendly manner of the dentist and his assistant, but most of all, she was impressed that the dentist had charged her father eight dollars, a very substantial sum of money in 1886.

Theresa's family laughed at her goal and it became the favorite story to tell the neighbors. No one ever thought Theresa would actually become a dentist. For one thing, dentistry was an almost unheard-of occupation for a woman at that time. Besides, the Hunt family were just farmers in Mountain Grove, Missouri, and they did not have the money to send her to dental school. Soon Theresa's ambitions were forgotten - by everyone but Theresa.

As was commonplace at that time, when Theresa graduated from the eighth grade, she obtained a teaching certificate and taught school for a few years. She lived with families and saved her salary of twenty dollars a month for future tuition at dental school. She also received valuable experience by working part time for a local dentist.

Finally, she had saved enough money to enter the Western Dental College in Kansas City, Missouri. She was surprised to find there were two other females in her class of sixty students. A few of the male students accepted the women, but many felt a woman's place was in the home and not the male-dominated dental profession. The dental school was located in a rough section of the city, and years later, Theresa laughed as she recalled how the male students would offer to walk the girls home and wanted to protect them, but could not accept them as fellow students. The men soon realized that in spite of the prejudice, the girls were determined to succeed. By graduation time, the girls had proven themselves worthy and gained the respect of their classmates.

While in school, Theresa also worked for a dentist in Kansas City. She later said he was lazy and she did most of his work, but the training was irreplaceable. In 1901, when Theresa graduated from the Western Dental College, she felt she was ready to conquer the world.

Upon graduation, Theresa was invited to work with a dentist in El Reno, Oklahoma. With very little money but a great deal of courage and determination, she boarded a train for Oklahoma Territory. In El Reno, she heard about the great need for a dentist in Watonga. So, packing her new Oklahoma Dental License No. 134, she boarded the northbound Rock Island train from El Reno to Watonga.

It was a dreary winter day, December 19, 1901, when Theresa arrived in the small frontier town. As the conductor helped her from the train, Theresa took a look at the town she had chosen to call home. Hastily constructed wooden buildings lined the main street, which was a dusty dirt road. On closer inspection, many of those buildings were saloons. It was not a pretty sight and Theresa's heart filled with despair.

Her reaction to the coarse town was much the same as that of an earlier resident, Mrs. Tom

Ferguson, who had arrived in 1892 with her husband, the pioneer editor and publisher of the *Watonga Republican* and later fourth Territorial Governor of Oklahoma. Elva Ferguson did not follow her first intuition to leave the bleak uncivilized settlement, but made Watonga her home for life. Theresa Hunt's first intuition also may have been to get back on that train and return to El Reno, but her courage and determination made her pick up her valise and start down the muddy road to the hotel.

Theresa's main concern was not how she would like the town but how would the town like her.

Dr. Theresa Hunt Tyler. Courtesy of the Oklahoma Dental Association.

Would this male dominated rough frontier town accept a lady dentist? She need not have worried. Watonga was ready for her, even before she was ready for Watonga.

Patients were waiting to see her even before she had checked into the hotel. The people of Watonga had been nine years without a dentist and they welcomed anyone who could pull a tooth - even a woman.

Since her newly ordered fancy dental chair had not arrived yet, Dr. Hunt treated patients in an unused hotel room, using a high-back dining room chair to seat them. She was very surprised and proud that she earned $18.00 on her first day in practice.

Later, she took a lease on an office suite in the Rose Building, a brick two-story building in the business district. She needed a place to practice while the building was being constructed, so accepted an offer to set up her equipment in the back room of Hooper's Drug Store. It was amazing how many patients, some holding their mouths, would fill the drug store while waiting their chance to see the dentist.

The Hoopers also offered Theresa a place to live. They were living in the Ferguson's home while the Governor and his family were living in Guthrie, the state capitol. Theresa rented the top floor for her living quarters. The room can still be seen at the T.B. Ferguson home, which is now a state museum.

She had not been in Watonga long when the realization hit her that not only did the people of Watonga accept and like her but she really liked the town of Watonga. For the first time, she did not have to fight for acceptance in her professional or personal life. She liked to hunt and fish and no one told her those were not ladylike hobbies. She entered two land lotteries and drew land both in Hobart and Grandfield. The society column in the *Watonga Republican* was as likely to report on Dr. Hunt going out of town to Hobart to work on her claim as it was to mention the attractive Dr. Hunt attending a social event.

The pretty young dentist had many suitors but none struck her fancy until 1902, when a handsome young man moved to town as a partner in a local mercantile store. Theresa and Homer Tyler found they had much in common. He was from Iowa and Theresa was born in Iowa, although she had moved to Missouri at an early age. In July 1903, the young couple took the train to Dallas where they were married. They set up living quarters behind the store.

In 1904, the store burned down in a fire that started in a nearby saloon and destroyed the entire city block. After the fire, the Tylers bought a farm and decided to move to the farm one half mile south of town. Theresa set up a dental office in the front room of the farm house. She kept her dental office in her home while raising their three children. In the winter time, the family would move to town and live in an apartment over the drug store.

Her son, Hugh, now in his 80s, remembered one winter in 1917 or 1918 when they did not move back to town. On Christmas Eve, his mother had planned to go to town to purchase items for the stockings and Christmas dinner. The worst blizzard in many years came up and it looked like there was no way to get to town. His mother told the boys to saddle Old May, the horse, and she would try to get to town. They saddled the horse and she climbed on, but Old May was stubborn and did not want to leave the warm stable. Each time they started for town Old May would return home. But Hugh's mother was as stubborn as the horse and finally she was able to get the horse to town. Theresa did not know who was happiest to return home that evening, she or Old May. The next day, the family had fresh oranges and peppermints in their stockings and each child got a pair of ice skates.

To supplement her income, Mrs. Tyler would travel by horse and buggy once a month to Eagle City. Eagle City is only a few miles from Watonga, but at that time it was a full day's trip. Taking one of the boys with her, they would travel one day, see patients the next day, and return home the following day. They would stay at the Maury Hotel, and she would use Mr. James' barber chair to examine patients.

People did not seem to mind going by buggy or horseback out to the farm to be treated. But as the children grew older, Dr. Tyler moved her office back to town. She was well respected as a dentist, but for some reason, after her marriage, the townspeople never again referred to her as "Doctor," but called her "Mrs. Tyler."

Her office was always busy, sometimes with people who wanted to just sit around and visit. When the farm families came to town, mothers would take their babies to the dental office to nurse them or change their diapers. Sometimes, people would bring their lunch and eat in her waiting room. Being a woman did not seem to be a detriment. In fact, many people came from surrounding towns for the sole purpose of being treated by a woman. One woman, for many years came to Dr. Tyler from Enid, passing many other dentist along the way.

Theresa often traveled to the nearby Indian camps around Watonga. The Indian might be dying, perhaps from old age, but the medicine man would decide the sickness was caused from the teeth and they would send for Dr. Tyler. She had to quit going because it was so difficult to explain to them that she was unable to help. She had a fine collection of Indian ware that was given to her in payment for her services.

Mrs. Tyler's fees for dental service stayed the same through the years. In 1941, for amalgam fillings she still charged one dollar for adults and fifty cents for children. Extractions were one dollar and gold crowns were five dollars. Usually, people paid in cash.

She did make one memorable exception. She made some false teeth for a man in town who claimed they did not fit. But he still wore them all the time. Theresa went to his house to collect the money. She asked to see the dentures, and when he handed her the teeth, she put them in her pocket and started to leave. The man became enraged and grabbed for his gun and blocked the door. Convinced she would be killed if she did not do so, she handed him back the teeth. She never was paid but gave up on trying to collect the bill.

Through the years she did have some funny experiences with people not realizing the dentist was a woman. One man came in holding his jaw and, thinking she was the dental assistant, said, "I want to see the dentist." When Mrs. Tyler said she was the dentist, he dropped his hand from his jaw and said, "It don't hurt no more."

Another time, a patient came in with a toothache. He was in pain and asked if she had any whiskey for him before she started to work. After downing half of a half-pint bottle, he rinsed his mouth and finished the bottle. He announced the tooth didn't hurt anymore and he didn't need it pulled after all. Then he got up from the dental chair and left.

Although there were three saloons in the block

where her office was located, Dr. Tyler kept a supply of whiskey on hand as an anesthetic, especially for the women who were not permitted in the saloons.

Patients usually only went to the dentist when the teeth were in bad condition. Dr. Tyler would try to save the tooth and would not pull a solid tooth. Occasionally, a patient would have a wisdom tooth that she was not strong enough to extract. In those cases, she would call in one of the local doctors to help. Dr. Tyler also did most of her own laboratory work such as making dentures.

Through the years Dr. Tyler saw many changes in dentistry and her beloved town of Watonga. In 1941, her family convinced her that after forty years it was time to give up her dental practice. Even so, many of her patients still came to her for consultation. In 1972, she died at the age of 94.

MIGNON LAIRD

Zigfield Showgirl

At the turn of the century, Mignon Laird appeared on the Pullman train car that her father used in his traveling medicine show. Later, in the 1920s, her name appeared in lights on Broadway when she appeared with the Zigfield Frolics. Still later, in 1967, an airport in Cheyenne, Oklahoma, was named the Mignon Laird Airport. The sixty year span demonstrates not only the progress in the last half century from rail to air travel, but also is a tribute to the career of a small town Oklahoma girl who became a success and her colorful pioneer family.

Mignon Laird was born to the smell of grease paint and grew up with the sounds of applause. She began her colorful theatrical career at the age of four months appearing on stage with her parents, Dr. H. C. Laird and his beautiful wife Elbertine.

The show was a traveling "med-opry" show, comparable to the old time medicine shows viewed in the movies, with entertainment and the selling of patent medicine after the show. But this show was much more. The talents of Dr. Laird, who actually was a medical doctor and a professional entertainer made towns all over Oklahoma eager for his visit.

Dr. Laird was a legend in early day Oklahoma both as a frontier doctor and a talented performer. His family represented a unique and elegant way of life in early day Oklahoma, as they toured the state in their own private railroad car that served as home, doctor's office, transportation, and the back drop for their evening performance.

Dr. Laird has been described in many ways: physician, medicine man, painless dentist, scholar, philosopher, musician, showman, pioneer, entrepreneur, and humanitarian. His wife Elbertine was described as dancer, singer, actress, musician, teacher, and pioneer. All these words fit this extraordinary couple, to whom Mignon Laird was born on April 7, 1904, at Mrs. Beales' Private Hospital in Oklahoma City.

Dr. Henri Laird was a medical doctor who obtained his degree in Missouri, with extended courses later from Johns Hopkins Hospital. He took his profession seriously, continuously reading medical journals and attending many refresher courses.

He was also a performer. Born in Illinois, he left home at an early age to follow the circus. He worked with the circus and various traveling shows until he had enough money to attend medical school. In St. Louis, he met and married an actress, Elbertine Hutchinson, who was also from a theatrical family.

In 1889, Dr. Laird brought his new medical bag and his bride to the newly opened Oklahoma Territory. He applied for a medical license and received License No. 82. Practicing medicine did not bring Dr. Laird enough income or enough excitement, so he and Elbertine began traveling around the state giving dramatic presentations and selling his patent medicine.

In 1892, a son, Clifford Irl, was born to the couple in St. Louis. They left the child with Elbertine's parents, fearing a traveling theatrical family life was not suitable for a small child.

When Mignon was born twelve years later, the couple were determined to keep her with them, and before long "Baby Mignon" was the star of the show. A favorite family story was the time Elbertine was on stage and could hear baby Mignon crying backstage. She realized the child was hungry but there was nothing she could do until the performance was

Mignon Laird, as a child star with the Laird's Refined Entertainment. Courtesy of the Archives and Manuscripts Division of the Oklahoma Historical Society.

over. She saw the baby sitter walking through the audience toward the back door. Suddenly, the crying stopped. After the final curtain, Elbertine rushed into the audience and found her baby tucked under the blanket of and nursing at the breast of an Indian woman, her own papoose on the cradle board beside her. The newspaper the next day carried the story and added they did not know how much Indian blood Mignon had but they had witnesses that she has Indian milk. As an adult, having spent her life living in hotels, Mignon liked to add to the story that she was a better Indian than many full-bloods, in that she never sat at a school desk and never lived in a house.

The Laird trio were welcomed and admired wherever they went. Dr. Laird was handsome and a compassionate doctor. Elbertine was beautiful and always fashionably dressed. Mignon was the idol of the younger set. Her beautiful clothes and stage accomplishments were the envy of the girls and the attraction for the young men. Mignon kept a diary in which she would write of the towns visited and the new friends she made in each location. Newspapers billed her as "the little friend to all the world."

The family was never in any one location long enough to put down roots but they claimed Cheyenne as their home because they established a homestead there in 1907. Traveling as they did, Mignon was never able to attend public school but her education did not suffer. She was educated by her father's extensive library, through family literary meetings, a private tutor when one was available, and daily lessons from her mother and father. Her extensive travels, also, gave her a more interesting and varied education than most children her age.

In 1919, her brother joined the show. Clifford and Mignon developed an exotic harp dance, in which Clifford would play the harp while Mignon danced around it.

In 1921, the Lairds made a decision that Mignon and Clifford deserved a chance at the "big time" in New York. With Elbertine as their chaperon they went east to seek their fortunes. Clifford only remained a short time, as his grandmother in St. Louis offered to buy him a harp studio. He accepted the offer and spent the rest of his life giving harp lessons in St. Louis.

Mignon became an immediate success when she made her debut in vaudeville. Although she was seventeen years old, her publicity review claimed her age as fourteen, making her appear even more gifted, and calling her "the teenage toast." She continued her exotic dance around the harp which was so special she had it copyrighted. She even took out an ad in the theatrical magazines warning any imitators.

Her really big success came when she was booked into the Zigfield Frolics, in a show headlined by another Oklahoman, Will Rogers. She received spotlight billing and a solo act with her harp. This was the height of her fame in the theater and lasted a little over a year.

In 1925 she opened at the famous Strand Roof in *Love Pirates*. She was thrilled when New York Governor M. E. Trapp brought a group of guests to see her dance. She appeared as a dancer at the Billy Rose Supper Club, and the Publix Theater Productions of New York City. She played the harp on luxury Caribbean cruise ships in 1931 and 1932.

The depression of the '30s brought hard times to everyone but Mignon was always able to find work. She appeared in Atlantic City in the Seashore Follies and she modeled for magazine covers. She played the harp in tea rooms and she crisscrossed the United States in vaudeville acts. Along with her harp, Mignon developed another act featuring a pet marmoset. Her mother, who had remained in New York with Mignon, opened a speech and elocution studio.

Mignon appeared in dancing roles for Warner Brothers Studios and in 1934 made her dramatic debut in *A Hunting We Will Go*.

She also had a featured role in a radio soap opera entitled *That's Life*. She had a beautiful speaking voice and continued on soap operas, dramatic shows, and situation comedies for many years.

In 1937, Mignon married Hylmar Johannson, although she kept the marriage a secret for several years. She never took her married name until after her father died in 1939. When they met Hylmar was a prop-man for the theater. During World War II, he was in the Merchant Marines. After the war he worked as a deep sea fisherman, at times owning several fishing fleets. Separated in 1959, the couple was divorced in 1971. Mignon worked with the federal authorities in declaring him an illegal alien and helped to have him deported from the United States.

Through the years, Dr. Laird had made his home in Oklahoma for most of the year, visiting his wife and daughter in New York for the remainder of the time. He had long since given up living in the railroad car, but lived in a recreational vehicle which he still used to travel over Southwestern Oklahoma. He was 84 and still seeing patients when he died on August 30, 1939. He was cremated as he instructed in his will. Mignon and Elbertine came back to Oklahoma to settle his estate and to take his ashes back to St. Louis for burial.

During the 1940s and 1950s Mignon continued with her radio career, playing the harp in tea rooms and performing her exotic dances. She developed a dance, called the Sin Dance, that was considered quite outrageous. She also studied the harp in master classes in New York City. She was very talented but had a reputation for being difficult to work with. She was temperamental and often late. She had a talent for attracting publicity and keeping her name in the newspapers. After her death, boxes and boxes of press notices were found in her apartment. Mignon took every job she could get, still hoping for another big break.

In 1954, her beloved mother Elbertine died. Mignon had her cremated and the ashes thrown into the Atlantic Ocean. Her brother Clifford Irl died in St. Louis in 1971.

After Elbertine's death, Mignon opened a dramatic school and taught her pupils dramatic reading, elocution, and acting. She also gave harp lessons. With her personality, she probably also imparted her knowledge of impersonation, dancing, and singing. She had always enjoyed living in hotels; the Hotel Cadillac in New York City was her favorite. Financial difficulties made it necessary to move to a small apartment. Mignon always kept her body in excellent shape and was still an active dancer when she was over sixty years of age.

In later years, Mignon was active in the former Zigfield Follies Girls Club. She attended the reunions and performed with them for benefits. At one point she worked as a companion for a former Zigfield Girl and accompanied her to Mexico.

One of the highlights of her life was returning to Cheyenne, in 1967, for the dedication of the Mignon Laird Airport. The airport was built on the land that her father homesteaded. Mignon sold the land to the city of Cheyenne for the airport. No matter where she was, Mignon always considered Cheyenne her home. She was a very dramatic person and the people of Cheyenne were very much in awe of her. She was at her theatrical best for the dedication and enjoyed the attention of the townsfolk.

At that point in time, she made a will leaving all her memorabilia to the Black Kettle Museum and the town of Cheyenne.

This was quite a contribution as it included all her costumes, her harp, and boxes and boxes of

Mignon Laird at about 60 years old, from the collection of Howard Metcalfe.

newspaper clippings tracing the entire career of Mignon and the Laird family. The collection also included Mignon's and Elbertine's diaries since the early 1900s, which detailed their life in show business and life in early day Oklahoma.

Mignon died in her apartment in New York City, May 21, 1980, at the age of 80. Even after death, she made one final dramatic appearance. On May 27, 1985, memorial services were held at the Mignon Laird Airport north of Cheyenne. Following instructions left by Mignon, after the memorial service a Native American dressed in full Indian regalia galloped across the airport scattering her ashes. The empty cremains container was tossed into the Washita River north of Cheyenne. It seemed an appropriate ending to someone who had spent a lifetime in theater.

Angie Debo. Courtesy of the Oklahoma Heritage Association.

ANGIE DEBO

Oklahoma's First Lady of History

Although proclaimed as the greatest historian Oklahoma ever produced, Angie Debo found the doors to a position in the history department of a university barred to women. Even with a Ph.D in history, Miss Angie never held a permanent teaching position in a university. She believed in writing the truth and recording history as it really happened - which made her, at times, Oklahoma's most controversial writer.

Miss Angie sat back in her chair and straightened her small body which bristled with emotion. She had always been known for being outspoken and at 95 years of age she saw no reason to change now.

"The only people who ever got famous writing about Oklahoma didn't know a thing about what they were writing about. Edna Ferber, who wrote *Cimarron* only spent 13 days here, and John Stinebeck who made "Okies" famous in *The Grapes of Wrath* never even set foot in the state. Those books are well know publicly but both are based on entirely false information."

Angie, who was well known for her integrity, continued, "Integrity is important because a book is just about the most permanent thing there is. I've tried to write the facts about Oklahoma and some of them are good, but I've also written more unpleasant things about Oklahoma than anybody who ever touched a typewriter."

Miss Angie was being interviewed for the 1988 award-winning PBS program about her life, entitled

"Indians, Outlaws, and Angie Debo."

All her life, Miss Angie sought truth and wrote it. She knew better than anyone else the history of Oklahoma; after all, she lived it!

Like so many of the pioneers she wrote about, Angie came to Oklahoma in a covered wagon. It was November 8, 1899, and she was just nine years old. From the beginning, she was intrigued with Oklahoma and hoped she would see an Indian along the way. The family settled in Marshall, Oklahoma, which was to be her home for the next 89 years.

As a child, she had a strong desire to obtain an education and have a career. She was bitterly disappointed when she reached high school age and there was no secondary school close enough for her to attend. At sixteen, she took an examination to teach and began teaching school near Douglas. She earned $35 a month, paid $2 a month board, and saved every penny she could to further her education. Finally, a high school opened near Marshall and Angie was in the first graduating class. She was twenty-three years old.

She continued to teach and paid her own college expenses, earning her bachelor's degree from the University of Oklahoma, and her Master's in history in 1924 from the University of Chicago.

She received her Ph.D. at the University of Oklahoma in 1933. Her dissertation, a history of the Choctaw Indians entitled *The Rise and Fall of the Choctaw Republic*, was published, to favorable reviews, and Angie was encouraged to start writing.

Angie graduated with honors and felt like she was close to reaching her ambition to become a college history teacher. She was shocked to find that the history field was closed, shut, and barred against women. In the 1920s, university faculties were almost exclusively male. Even with a Ph.D., Angie

Debo would never hold a prominent position in the history department of a university.

With no teaching jobs available, Angie decided to go home to Marshall and build a career in a field where she knew she had a chance - writing.

Angie signed a book contract with the University of Oklahoma Press for a new field of study - The History of the American Indian. Neither the University nor Angie had any idea what scandals her research would uncover. What was to become Angie Debo's most important book was also to uncover Oklahoma's most shameful period of history. The book deals with the liquidation of the Five Civilized Tribes, the division of their lands, and the exploitation that resulted. Angie exposed the corruption of the politicians, courts, newspapers, and even the churches, which took the land away from the Indians.

When she began her research, Angie did not know that such corruption existed, but true to her integrity, once she started she did not feel she could honestly back out.

Dr. Edward Everett Dale, head of the history department at the University of Oklahoma, obtained a letter from the Commissioner of Indian Affairs that opened all files and records. Angie spent months in Washington, DC, in the basement of the Interior Building. She traveled all over Oklahoma going through old musty files in the courthouses. She began to find more and more information and it got worse all the time.

She said, "Everything I touched about that story was slimy." For the first time in her life, Angie felt afraid. She would look behind her in dark corridors and jump at the slightest noise. Her friend and fellow historian, Dr. Arrell Gibson said, "I believe that Angie was in danger. She was finding out information about well-respected people in the state that had been kept hidden for many years."

Angie found that the Dawes Commission had lied about the Indian acceptance to carving up their tribal lands and giving them individual allotments. The Indians were in bitter opposition, as they knew it would destroy their way of life. When they were moved West, the treaties they signed guaranteed the right to remain a nation. The allotment was an attempt to abolish the tribal system. Many Indians refused to register with the Dawes Commission, some were intimidated into signing, and other names were forged.

With the discovery of oil, came also the discovery that those individual allotments were on top of oil. Each Indian had to deal with a legal system of private ownership, contracts, deeds, mortgages, powers of attorney and oil leases. The average Indian could not read or write English and was totally helpless as the white men robbed them of their land, systematically, through the courts. In less than 20 years, eighty percent of the Indian land was in white hands. Land worth millions was purchased for five, ten, and fifteen cents an acre. Under the individual allotment system, children also received allotments. The parents did not understand the procedure of guardianship, so professional guardians arose, who robbed the children of their land.

The worst frauds were committed against the orphans. The Indians had always cared for their orphans by shared family life or orphan asylums which they established. Speculators searched for names of orphans, whose allotments could be placed under guardianship. Lists were supplied to judges and politicians in exchange for political favors. A guardian might have as many as twenty to thirty orphans placed under his authority. Angie had always been an admirer of Kate Barnard, the first Oklahoma Commissioner of Charities and Corrections. Angie remembered that Kate's investigation into the federal money sent for Indian orphans had caused the state government to discontinue funds for the Department of Charities and Corrections.

The men charged with protecting the Indians grew rich while plundering their land. Top leaders in the state and powerful figures all the way to Washington, DC, were connected with the scandals. And Angie named them. Prominent names like former Governor Charles Haskell, Senator Robert Owen, and Tams Bixby, the chairman of the Dawes Commission.

It was so tempting and so easy, as the prevalent attitude was, "So what, these are just Indians." Angie detailed some cases that went as far as kidnapping, murder and embezzlement by businessmen.

As Angie finished each chapter, she would read it to her mother, who would shake her head and say, "They will never publish this book." She was right. When Angie delivered the completed manuscript to Dr. Dale and the OU Press, they refused to publish it due to the prominent names it contained. The contract was torn up. Years later, Angie would say, "I violated history. I told the truth."

The OU press did help her find a publisher and four years later, in 1940, the book was eventually published by Princeton University Press. *And Still The Waters Run* received wonderful reviews across the country, but not in Oklahoma where very few people were aware of its existence.

This was a time of discouragement and financial difficulties for Angie. She worked as a substitute teacher in high schools near Marshall and was pastor of the local Methodist Church. She was hired by the Federal Writers Project to write a chapter on the history of Oklahoma, but when the book was printed a different chapter appeared, although it had her name as author. Angie was very upset, as the article was full of mistakes and misspelled words. She wrote articles for *Harper's Magazine* and reviewed books for the *New York Times*.

Then she received a grant and wrote the highly successful history of the Creek Indians, *The Road To Disappearance*, which was published by the University of Oklahoma Press in 1941.

Angie wrote thirteen books and over a hundred articles and book reviews. She wrote about Oklahoma settlers in *Oklahoma, Footloose and Fancy Free* which was issued on November 8, 1949, the date that marked the fiftieth anniversary of the Debo family arriving in Oklahoma. Her only work of fiction, *Prairie City*, was almost nonfiction, as she used her hometown of Marshall as a prototype of an Oklahoma frontier town. Prairie City Days have been celebrated in Marshall each year since 1968, in honor of Miss Angie. Her best seller *Geronimo* was written and published when Angie was 87 years old.

Late in life, Angie was to receive much deserved recognition from her beloved state of Oklahoma. In 1983, she was given the University of Oklahoma's Distinguished Service Citation. April, 1985, was declared Angie Debo Month by Governor George Nigh. Her portrait, painted by Charles Banks Wilson, was hung at the state capitol. She was the first woman so honored. The artist portrayed her as a woman of authority and excellence. Angie was very pleased with his portrayal. In a letter to him she said, "It is not beautiful. That is correct. I have never been beautiful... but it shows the characteristic that I now know dominated my life... it was drive. It carried me though my whole lifetime."

In 1988, she was given an "award for scholarly distinction" from the American Historical Association which recognized her career of 52 years. This honor had been conferred on only six other scholars, all of whom were men. She had finally risen above the discrimination barrier. The award was announced in December of 1987, but Angie was too ill to attend the ceremony in Washington, D. C., so Governor Henry Bellmon came to Marshall and conferred the award on her with family and friends present.

Miss Angie turned 98 on January 30, 1988. She died on February 21, 1988, and was buried in her beloved Marshall. Governor Bellmon ordered the state flags to be flown at half mast. The little girl, who at 11 years of age, dedicated her life to service and integrity, was honored at 98 as one of Oklahoma's most outstanding citizens.

Miss Alice Robertson presided over the U.S. House of Representatives in 1921. Courtesy of the Archives and Manuscripts Division of The Oklahoma Historical Society.

MISS ALICE ROBERTSON

She Kept House for the Nation

In 1922, in answer to a reporter's question as to how she felt about her term in office as a United States Representative, Miss Alice Robertson replied, "If you asked a housekeeper, what do you think she would say? I've been busy keeping house for the nation just like a woman would her own home – busy, busy, busy, every day, in every way, without any outstanding thing to show for it."

A popular T-shirt saying of today expresses the theme, "A woman's place is in the house - and in the senate". This is not a new idea - Miss Alice Robertson proved the truth back in 1920 when she was elected Oklahoma's first and only woman to serve in the United States House of Representatives. She was only the second woman in the entire United States to hold such an office. While a representative, Miss Alice presided over the House several times, making her the first woman in the history of the world to preside over a legislative body. And yet, Miss Alice herself believed that a woman's place was in the family home and not in public office.

Although she achieved many honors and world wide fame, her deepest desire was to stay at home and fulfill what she believed to be a woman's ultimate goal, to be a wife and mother. A bitter opponent of women's suffrage, fearing it would destroy the family, Miss Alice felt it was her duty to protect family values by running for office.

These feelings were characterized in 1922, in her answer to a reporters's question as to how she felt about her term in office. She said, "If you asked a housekeeper, what do you think she would say? I've been busy keeping house for the nation just like a woman would her own home - busy, busy, every day, in every way, without any outstanding thing to show for it."

Walking around Washington, D.C., in her old fashioned long black skirt and thick cotton stockings, the United States Representative from Indian Territory created a lot of attention in style conscious Washington. Miss Alice was quite a social and political enigma, both in Washington and back in Oklahoma.

She was sixty-six years old, a former missionary, successful businesswoman, and former postmaster. She was a Republican in a Democratic district. She was a woman and this was the first year women were allowed to vote; however, she had campaigned against woman suffrage and had even been vice-president of the state Anti-Suffrage League. Alice was a reluctant politician who believed that a woman's ultimate goal was to be a wife and mother. Yet she never married.

Miss Alice gave her entire life to public service, although she only held office for two years. During those two years she became known around the world as a woman who always kept to her beliefs. Her platform was , "I am a Christian, I am an American, and I am a Republican." Her campaign slogan was, "I cannot be bought, I cannot be sold, I cannot be intimidated." Voters rarely take such campaign promises seriously, but they knew that Miss Alice meant exactly what she said.

Even her campaign for office was quite unusual. With only $2,940.00 to spend, both the two Muskogee newspapers against her election, and her belief that it was undignified for a woman to make speeches in public, Miss Alice devised an original way of getting votes. What would now be called "creative advertising" was a "want-ad" system of promoting her campaign in the classified section of the district's daily papers. She published her own writings, little paragraphs in which she set out her view on politics and other matters, including the menu of the day for her Sawokla cafeteria. One such ad read:

> Watermelons better every day. Fried chicken extra good tonight. Our campaign is going very well, even if we are not neglecting our customers.

Another read:

> We do not find business as usual, "but better than usual," and we wonder vaguely if the increase is caused by a pardonable curiosity to see the one and only woman candidate for Congress. Lots of hot soup today, and catfish, fried brown. Sweet potatoes, getting sweeter every day; pole beans, boiled with bacon in the pot; corn bread, made from white meal; buttermilk; cherry pie.

Miss Robertson's campaign advertisements soon rivaled the local news for public interest, as readers first turned to the Want Ads "to see what the woman candidate says today."

Although Miss Alice found it unwomanly to make campaign speeches, she found it neighborly to personally meet as many people as possible. At the cafeteria, she went from table to table greeting diners and handing out small cards that read:

> There are already more lawyers and bank-

ers in Congress than are needed. The farmers need a farmer, I am a farmer. The women need a woman to look after their new responsibilities. The soldier boys need a proven friend. I promise few speeches, but faithful work. You can judge my promise by my past performance."

Alice M. Robertson

Her campaign tactics worked. In the primary, from a field of five candidates, she received the majority of all votes cast. She won the general election, although by less than 300 votes. Her victory could be attributed to her popularity among the women, the soldiers, the Native Americans, and the fact that a Republican landslide hit Oklahoma and most of the nation. Warren Harding won the Presidency, and in traditionally Democratic Oklahoma, Republicans elected five out of eight members of Congress and sent a Republican to the Senate.

Before she even took the oath of office, Miss Alice's election attracted national attention. It was inconceivable to many that an anti suffragist and one with so little political experience would be elected. One newspaper even suggested that she run the House restaurant and let the other Representatives run the House. She was interviewed extensively on her beliefs that women should remain at home and not be bothered by politics.

Her unusual appearance also attracted a lot of attention. She always wore black, usually a long skirt and thick cotton stockings. Asked if she intended to shorten her skirts to the fashionable length of the twenties, she replied that all her dresses would be the same length as usual, to the ankles. As for silk stockings, she had never owned a pair and never intended to. In her opinion, women who wore stockings were extravagant, and short skirts or low bodices were disgusting. Once she refused to cross her feet for a photographer, saying, "There are some things I will not do. I was raised never to cross my feet and I am going to stay that way."

One rather kindly newspaper reporter described her as an unpretentious dresser but many described her as "old fashioned." The Washington Herald, wrote, "One never quite knows what Miss Alice has on. Her costume is always black, and of a cut behind the prevailing mode, but it somehow suits the snow-white hair and matronly style of the lady from Oklahoma, who is called "the Jane Addams of the South."

Headlines were made when Miss Alice, America's only woman member of Congress, met Lady Astor, England's only member of Parliament. Newspapers emphasized the contrast in the appearance of the two women "Lady Astor, a graceful figure in fawn-colored crepe, with pearls, long gloves and a plumed picture hat - Miss Alice with her plain black dress, cotton stockings, and sensible shoes." However, the two women regarded each other with mutual respect and genuine affection. Miss Alice regarded the meeting as one of the highlights of her life. She wrote her sister Augusta in Oklahoma, "More wonderful things have happened than you can imagine. God has given me more than I ever dreamed possible could come into my life. Imagine me being escorted into dinner by Lord Astor."

Always a puzzle to the newspaper reporters, Miss Alice was generally regarded a kind, thoughtful, spirited person who could always be counted on to vote her convictions, even at the cost of losing votes.

She incurred the wrath of women when she voted against the "Maternity Bill," one of the early welfare measures in which the Government was to furnish instructions on child care and personal hygiene and prenatal care to women. The bill was supported by the state Boards of Health, the American Association of University Women, the General Federation of Women's Clubs, the National Board of the Y.W.C.A., the National Consumers' League, the National Federation of Business and Professional Women, the National Women's Christian Temperance Union, the National League of Women Voters, Council of Jewish Women, and even an organization of which Miss Alice was an ardent member - the Daughters of the American Revolution. Against this impressive array, she stood her ground. Her opposition was the control of the Federal Government in family matters. She said, "Let the Federal Government get its foot in the door and there will be no end to it."

Even more shocking to the folks back home in Oklahoma was Miss Alice's opposition to a Veteran's bonus. A staunch supporter of American soldiers, Miss Alice helped recruit Troops L and M of Theodore Roosevelt's Rough Riders. In 1916, when 15,000 soldiers passed through Muskogee enroute to the Mexican border, Miss Alice met the trains and provided the men with postcards, sandwiches, and milk from her farm. Her devotion was especially apparent during WWI, when over 5,000 soldiers ate at her cafeteria where a soldier or member of a soldier's family was never charged for a meal. Soldiers across the United States knew if they needed help they could always turn to Miss Alice of Muskogee, Oklahoma. These same soldiers were stunned and incredulous when they learned that Miss Alice opposed Veterans benefits, saying a soldier's patriotism should not have a price.

Voters should not have been surprised by Miss

Alice's reaction to these bills, because she had always been against the intrusion of government and any extension of state welfare. People should have to make their own way in life as she had done.

Throughout her childhood and young life, she had led a hand-to-mouth existence, learning the value of hard work and sacrifice.

Miss Alice was descended from a long line of strong women who had devoted their lives to service to their country.

Her grandmother, Sarah Elizabeth Worcester, had left a comfortable life in New England to join her husband Samuel as one of the first missionaries to the Cherokee Indians in Georgia in 1825. He gained fame as the translator and printer of books and parts of the Bible in the Cherokee language. Under his supervision, a printing press was imported and the Cherokee alphabet invented by Sequoyah was printed, making the Cherokees the first literate Indian nation. He later was imprisoned for refusing to swear allegiance to the state of Georgia against the Cherokees, pledging to keep his faith with the people he served. In 1835, the Worcester family made the famed trek of the "Trail of Tears" with the Cherokees to the wild domain known as Indian Territory. Sarah's life was never easy but one of dedication and perseverance.

Ann Eliza Worcester Robertson, the mother of Alice, was born in the Cherokee nation in Georgia, and made the journey to Indian Territory as a small child. Educated at the Vermont Academy, she then returned to Park Hill, Oklahoma, where she taught school. She married the Reverend William S. Robertson and their lives were spent as missionaries and educators to the Creek Indians. Ann Eliza translated the Bible into the Creek language for which scholarly work she was given an honorary

Ph.D from Wooster College in 1892. She was the first woman in the United States to have a Ph.D.

Alice was born January 2, 1854, at the Tullahassee Mission. At the age of seven, her family was forced to flee from the Mission because of the Civil War. The Civil War years were spent moving from place to place in Kansas, Wisconsin and Illinois. In 1866, the family returned and rebuilt the destroyed mission.

At seventeen, Alice was sent to Elmira College in New York, studying English, history, and civics. However, due to a lack of money and the necessity of her helping earn money to educate her younger brothers and sisters, Alice was forced to leave school before her graduation. In 1866, on the fortieth anniversary of the day she should have graduated, she was awarded an honorary Master's Degree from Elmira College. She wrote Augusta that she still remembered having her head in her pillow, crying her eyes out that her classmates were graduating without her.

After leaving Elmira, she took a clerkship in the Indian Office of the Department of Interior. At nineteen, she was the youngest and the only woman clerk in the service. She wrote her family of her homesickness but she managed to study shorthand, typing and domestic science.

In 1888, she became secretary to Captain R. H. Pratt, superintendent of the Carlisle Indian School in Pennsylvania. Soon afterward, she received word that Tullahassee Mission had burned to the ground. She returned to Oklahoma, but not before she made arrangements for twenty-five of the older students to attend Carlisle School.

When she returned, she found that her father had died and her mother was trying to conduct a small school in the ashes of the burned mission and was heavily in debt. She helped her mother with the school and was asked by the Presbyterian Board of Home Missions to come east and help raise money for Indian Missions. For two years, she traveled from church to church, college to college, giving fund raising talks.

In 1884, Alice decided she had raised enough money for a beginning, and it was time to return to Indian Territory and establish the schools. Nuyaka Mission School was opened in 1884 with Alice's sister Augusta as superintendent. She began her own boarding school, Minerva Boarding School for Girls, in her home in Muskogee. She and her mother ran the school and Alice oversaw the marriage of many of her girls to wealthy men in the community. At the age of thirty-five, Miss Alice resigned herself to the fact that she would never marry. It was not that she did not have many offers but she felt a strong obligation to her mother and to carry on the work they had started. She also said, "the kind of man who would want a woman like me would not be the kind of man I would be interested in."

The school grew and in 1894 the Presbyterian Board of Home Missions took over the school, operating it under the name of Henry Kendall College. Miss Alice was the first professor of English and also held the chair of Civics and History. Some years later, the school was moved to Tulsa, and in 1920 it became the University of Tulsa.

To help supplement her income and care for her aging mother, Miss Alice took in boarders and also operated a photographic gallery on the side. In 1889, she was also employed as a stenographer with the Indian Commission sent out to negotiate with the Cherokee Nation for the session of the Cherokee Outlet.

Another event that was to have a profound effect on her life was being named a member of the celebrated Mohonk Conference which held annual meetings to address Indian problems at Lake Mohonk in the Catskills. In 1891, Miss Alice was addressing the conference of some hundred editors, writers, teachers, and government officials on the education of the Five Civilized Tribes. In the audience was Theodore Roosevelt, at that time U. S. Civil Service Commissioner, who was very impressed with the missionary from Indian Territory. This was the beginning of a long friendship. They exchanged letters, Miss Alice helped to recruit soldiers for the Spanish American War, and Roosevelt paid tribute to Alice Robertson in his book, *The Rough Riders.*

In 1900, she became United States School Supervisor for Creek Schools and served until 1905. She looked after the appointment of teachers, visited schools, audited accounts, prepared statistics, made quarterly and annual reports, and each summer handled two normal schools. Her work required her to drive with horse and buggy in all kinds of weather, throughout the Creek country into sparsely settled communities, but she was never molested. There were few hotels and she accepted the hospitality of Indian friends who were always glad to welcome her.

When Roosevelt became President, in 1905, one of his first appointments was Miss Alice as Postmistress of Muskogee, making her the first woman to hold that position in a first class post office. She was now fifty years old. She held the position as postmistress until 1913. A Muskogee newspaper described her as "Muskogee's postmaster, Miss Alice Robertson, who can bake bread or 'throw the lariat,' who can write a story or make a speech, who can decorate a church or talk practical politics."

In 1910, Miss Alice fulfilled her dream of building a home of her own in the country at historic Agency Hill, now known as Honor Heights, three miles west of Muskogee. There she built Sawokla, a spacious house of native rock and shingles, surrounded by oak trees, and looking out over the Arkansas River to the site of the old Tullahassee Mission where she was born. Sawokla was a Creek name meaning "gathering place" and it soon lived up to the name as the site of many events.

In downtown Muskogee she also opened the Sawokla Cafeteria, which began as a club for working girls, with a reading room, showers, and country style food sold at moderate prices. It soon became so popular that it was expanded into a profitable public cafeteria. Food for the cafeteria came from the Sawokla farm where Miss Alice kept a large herd of Jersey and Guernsey cattle, a thousand chickens, and several big vegetable gardens. It was from this cafeteria that Miss Alice began feeding soldiers and supplying canteens during World War I, and the 1920 successful campaign for U.S. Representative.

And it was to Sawokla that Miss Alice returned after being defeated for her bid for a second term of office. Her defeat was no surprise. With the loss of the veterans' support, she knew she was in trouble. But as she explained, she voted against every appropriation she felt could be handled without Government involvement, and she prided herself on standing up for her beliefs though she knew her constituency was against her. She was not bitter about the loss and remarked, "I've been Cinderella at sixty-nine, but now, the pumpkin is round the corner waiting to whisk me back."

After her return to Oklahoma, everything seemed to run downhill. Sawokla Cafeteria, sold in 1921, had gone out of business. President Harding waived the Civil Service regulations "in just recognition of her very great merits" for her to accept a post with the new Veterans' Hospital in Muskogee. This was met with opposition from local political opponents who challenged the Civil Service rules and her opposition to the Veterans' bonus. In less than two years, she was dismissed from her salaried post and named "spiritual advisor" to the patients without pay. Indignantly, she left the hospital, announcing that she was going to Oklahoma City to become state president of the Women's Coolidge for President Club. She said she was not worried because her new job paid no salary. "God will take care of me. I have always done right."

In 1925 she opened a tearoom at Sawokla Farm, but during one of her absences the building burned to the ground. With part of the insurance money, she opened another tearoom in Muskogee but it failed. The *Muskogee Daily News* asked her to write a column entitled, "Miss Alice Says," and to go to Washington occasionally as their correspondent. But after only a few months, the *Muskogee Daily News* failed.

Miss Alice began to hold sales in the spring and fall, offering homemade jellies, preserves and pickles, as well as many of her heirlooms and treasurers - linens, old lace, dishes, and glassware, and some Indian artifacts which had been given to her years before. With time on her hands, Miss Alice began to sort books and papers, preparing to write "the family history of a hundred years of missionary work among the Cherokees and Creeks."

Relatives and friends heard of her plight and contributed welcome but inadequate sums of money and gifts. In 1927, the Oklahoma Historical Society elected Miss Robertson to the position of research assistant at $125.00 a month. She was proud of the recognition but the salary was not a living wage in pre-depression years. She added to it by writing feature stories about early Oklahoma for the *Sunday Phoenix* at Muskogee, at five dollars a week.

Ironically, during this time of financial necessity, honors were being bestowed upon her from all over the state. Portraits were being painted and unveiled, schools and university dormitories were named after her, trees were planted in her honor, and Will Rogers made her the subject of his nationally syndicated column "All I know is just what I read in the newspapers" in an article entitled "Ain't Old People Lovely?" The Oklahoma Federation of Business and Professional Women's Clubs selected her as Oklahoma's most famous woman in a pageant presented at their national convention. In 1929, she was named to the Oklahoma Hall of Fame. Just as her whole life had been a series of contradictions, now in her last years she was living in poverty while being recognized as a great stateswoman.

Her darkest hour was yet to come for in 1929, the Oklahoma legislature failed to appropriate the funds for her small salary. A small group of supporters led by millionaire oilman and philanthropist Lew Wentz formed an organization for the purpose of providing an annuity of $200.00 a month for the remainder of Alice Robertson's life. She was thrilled when the organization made plans to place a statue of her near Sequoyah in Statuary Hall in the national capitol. She never knew that after the death of Will Rogers, in 1935, Oklahoma voted that his statue should stand beside Sequoyah's to represent the state.

Early in 1931, Miss Alice was hospitalized with throat cancer and died on July 1, 1931. She had been friends to the Indians, the soldiers, and Presidents and Kings, and her life was a link from the missionary pioneer to the modern day. President Herbert

Hoover described her well in a telegram of sympathy sent to her sister Augusta: "The death of your sister, Alice Mary Robertson, former Representative in Congress and a leader in education of Indian youth, ends the career of a woman whose ancestry, idealism and outlook on life linked the pioneer past with the progress of the present. Hers was a life rich in usefulness. I wish to express to you and members of the family my deepest sympathy."

In his column "Will Rogers Says:" the famous humorist said, "You remember I told you there was some awful good dead republicans. Well, the finest one of 'em all went yesterday, ex-congresswoman Alice Robertson of Oklahoma." He concluded his column with, "She was a fine old soul, too fine for politics."

THE HARVEY GIRLS

Will Rogers once said, "Fred Harvey kept the West supplied with food and wives." Railroad travel and the Harvey House Restaurants located along the Santa Fe Railroad made some big changes in Oklahoma. Not only was being a Harvey House waitress a respectable means of employment for Oklahoma girls but it also brought young women from the East to Oklahoma. Many of them remained in the state. The legendary Harvey Girls are considered by many historians as the "Women who civilized the West."

The train whistle sounded loudly, echoing across the quiet prairie. A torrent of black smoke could be seen from a distance, warning the station master that the Santa Fe train was on schedule and would pull into the station at Hugo, Oklahoma, in about ten minutes. A gong sounded inside the small cafe and the waitresses immediately sprang into action.

The engineer had already telegraphed ahead; they could expect twelve passengers to dine in the lunch room and ten to have lunch in the dining room. The travelers had already made their choices from the extensive menu the train porter had given them, and the aroma of roast beef and Long Island duckling filled the building.

The Irish linen tablecloths were in place, the tables were set with fine china and crystal water glasses, and the coffee cups were arranged in exactly the proper position. All that was left to do was to place the frosted silver pitchers of ice water on the table and set the first course of fruit or salad at each place. The girls hurriedly completed the last minute assignments, made a quick check of their uniforms and arranged themselves at their assigned tables or stood in a row by the front door. They knew precisely what their duties were and they were ready; after all, they were the finest waitresses in the West. They were Harvey Girls!

The passengers that alighted from the train were hot, tired, and hungry. They had spent hours in the parching Oklahoma heat, riding through the desolate Indian Territory. They had not seen a house, let alone a town in hours. The frowns on their faces turned to smiles, as they were greeted by the friendly waitresses.

Taking their seats, they were immediately poured glasses of ice water and the waitress took their drink orders. The diners did not notice the waitress turning their coffee cups and were amazed that the drink girl, without asking, poured them the correct beverage, coffee, iced tea, hot tea or milk. They never suspected the cup code that was used in all Harvey establishments. A cup right side up in the saucer meant coffee; upside down, hot tea; upside down and tilted against the saucer, iced tea; upside down and off the saucer, milk. This was just one of many of Fred Harvey's little tricks for assuring faster smoother service, in feeding trainloads of passengers.

The menu selection was astounding. Here in the middle of nowhere they had could begin their meal with fresh fruit, clam chowder or fresh blue point oysters. Selections, in the dining room, for the main course might include roast Long Island duckling, prime rib of beef, filet mignon, or sugar cured ham. The lunch room would offer salad, sandwich, and soup selections, along with several plate lunch choices including fried chicken, minute sirloin steak or Hungarian goulash. Deserts were mouth-watering arrays of pies, cakes, cobblers and homemade ice creams. The meals were coordinated along the line, so that a passenger traveling for several days would not have the same menu. If they had chicken on Monday for lunch, the evening meal would be beef, and Tuesday they might be served fish.

The food, service and atmosphere were a far cry from the greasy spoon cafes that train travelers were used to finding in the railroad towns. They could also be assured that the meal would be served promptly and they could relax and enjoy themselves, knowing they would be finished before the scheduled departure time.

The Harvey Girls were not only efficient but they were neat pretty young ladies, usually between eighteen and thirty years of age. It was obvious they were of good character, not like many of the coarse waitresses and saloon girls found in the West. In talking with the waitresses, the travelers found that girls had come from all over the county, usually the East and Midwest. The question always arose: what had made these girls come West to live and work in frontier railroad settlements filled with saloons, cattlemen, prostitutes and outlaws. The answer was simple; Fred Harvey and his advertisement in their local newspaper.

Although it was becoming more acceptable for young ladies to work outside the home in the late 1800s and early 1900s, it was difficult to find suitable types of employment. Unless educated to be a teacher or a nurse, there was a limited number of respectable occupations open to women. So when the following advertisement appeared in many eastern and Midwestern newspapers, it was read with great interest:

Wanted: Young women, 18 to 30 years of age, of good moral character, attractive and intelligent, as waitresses in Harvey Eating Houses on the Santa Fe Railroad in the West. Wages $17.50 per month with room and board. Liberal tips customary. Experience not necessary. Write Fred Harvey, Union Depot, Kansas City, Missouri.

Fred Harvey had been warned, no one would answer such an ad, but the response from attractive intelligent women of good character was overwhelming. For these women to pack up and go west to areas that were sparsely settled was indeed an act of courage and of a true pioneer. Thus began the first "Harvey Girls," waitresses from the 1800s to the 1950s who became legends in the West.

The first ad was placed in 1883 although Harvey eating places did not appear in Oklahoma until 1896. In 1896, the first Harvey House Cafes and lunchrooms in Oklahoma were opened in Afton, Francis, Hugo, Madill, Okmulgee, and Tulsa. In 1903, the first dining room in Oklahoma was opened in Guthrie, and in 1910 another dining room opened in Waynoka. By the time the Harvey Houses reached Oklahoma, Fred Harvey had become an institution in the West.

Fred Harvey was only fifteen years old in 1850, when he emigrated to the United States from London. With only ten dollars in his pocket, he stepped ashore in New York City, and found a two dollar a week job as a dishwasher in an exclusive restaurant. The hardworking young boy soon upgraded his status to waiter. When he was not busy, and on his days off work, he followed the chefs around, learning all he could about food preparation and service. His dream was to someday own his own exclusive restaurant.

At the age of twenty-two, he opened his first

cafe in St. Louis. During the Civil War, his partner ran off with all the money, Harvey was stricken with typhoid, and the business was lost. He got a job as a mail clerk for the Hannibal and St. Joseph, Missouri Railroad and saw for himself how terrible the eating establishments were along the railroad lines. He became quite upset at the dirty cafes, the poorly prepared food and the poor service.

With his experience and knowledge of restaurants and railroads, Fred Harvey thought he could make a difference. He and the Santa Fe Railroad officials worked out an agreement for a chain of restaurants along the Santa Fe with a guarantee that trains would stop at the restaurants. The railroad would provide the building for the restaurant, furnish free freighting of food, ice, coal, water, and transportation for employees. As the cafe owner, Harvey would supply the equipment, workers, and food. Train crews could eat at half price. This was an arrangement that worked out satisfactorily to both parties. In just a few years, Fred Harvey changed railroad travel forever by serving to railroad passengers high quality meals in elegant surroundings.

Fred Harvey found the only thing wrong with his elegant restaurants was the service. The waiters he hired were mostly burly hash slingers who were rude to the customers. They might just as likely get in a fight with the customers or get drunk and not show up for work. Thus he came up with the idea of hiring women. His women would not just be waitresses but would project an image. They were never to be called waitresses but were to be called "Harvey Girls." Although the food made the Santa Fe and the Harvey Houses popular, many say it was the Harvey Girls who really captured the attention of the nation.

It was very exciting and flattering to be chosen

a Harvey Girl. The girls came from different backgrounds and ways of life. Although many applied

Harvey Girls in Hugo in approximately 1920 are Virginia Akins and unidentified coworker.

because of economic necessity, others thought of this as an opportunity to leave home and see the country. Independence and spunk were not characteristics that were greatly admired in women of that time and few opportunities existed for single women to be on their own. To become a Harvey Girl offered a chance for adventure within the confines of a strict, regulated system. Under the protective arm of the Fred Harvey system, they were told where to live, what to wear, what time to go to bed, and even who to date. They were expected to act like Harvey Girls, twenty-four hours a day.

Fred Harvey demanded a high standard of performance and sought young women who were strong, healthy, independent, and unafraid of hard work. Being a Harvey Girl involved a lot of close scrutiny. Applicants had to go through a very extensive interview and background check. Once accepted, they were sent West for training. Many insisted that training was far worse than any army boot camp. There a new recruit was to learn "The Harvey Way."

Each woman signed a contract for at least six months, agreeing to follow all employee instructions, obey employee rules, go wherever she was assigned to work, and to not marry during the term of the contract. They were expected, if necessary, to put in ten hour days and six and seven day weeks.

The girls lived in dormitories, two to a room, under the vigilant eye of a house mother. Curfew was at ten o'clock during the week and at twelve o'clock on Saturday night.

They wore basically black dresses with white aprons, with or without bibs, black shoes and stockings, and a white ribbon in the hair. The head waitress was recognized by her all-white uniform, and a manager wore a white blouse and black skirt. The uniform was to be kept spotless. If a spot or spill occurred, the uniform was to changed immediately. There was to be no nail polish, no gum, no profanity, and skirts were to be worn a certain length from the floor.

When a train was not imminent, the girls were to keep busy folding the heavily starched cloth napkins, polishing the silver or dusting the premises. Managers would put on white gloves and run their hands along surfaces, looking for dust. Each girl was expected to keep her station up to standard. Tables, chairs, countertops, salt and pepper shakers were all to be spotless and ready for the next diners.

Fred Harvey was famous for making unexpected spot checks along the line. He would take his white handkerchief from his breast pocket and check for dust. He was known to yank the table linen and all the dishes off a table if the cloth was not smoothly ironed or the table not properly set in "the Harvey manner." Each plate had to be an equal distance from the table edge, the silverware placed just so, water glasses exactly the same distance from the knives, and the napkins folded precisely. The sight of a chipped dish or wilted flowers could turn him into a rage. A silver pitcher with fingerprints or smudges or containing melted ice or luke warm water would be poured on the floor. He was also just as quick to compliment or lavish praise on the staff.

The restrictions might have been stifling to a few of the women but to most that was just part of "the Harvey way." The pay and the tips were more than adequate. Their room and uniforms were furnished and the free food was the best. Most girls were able to send money home or save quite a nest egg. The incentive was good. The girls started at the lowest station and the most undesirable locations so they worked hard to move up to head waitress or manager. As head waitress, the pay was better, they had a private room in the dormitory, and it carried a great deal of prestige.

The girls most of all enjoyed the friendships and camaraderie that developed through their somewhat secluded way of life. In the evenings they might relax in their rooms, or play games and sing songs or take walks together. They would decorate for holidays and take part in town activities such as ice cream socials and local dances.

Men were not allowed in the dormitories but there was a courting parlor to receive gentlemen callers. Although the girls signed a contract not to get married, marriage was always on the horizon. The contract was easily broken, usually with Fred Harvey's blessings. Literally thousands of Harvey girls ended their restaurant careers by marrying men in western towns. During the height of the Harvey Houses, it was amazing how many children were born, in the West, who were named either "Fred" or "Harvey."

Harvey Girls tended to marry men of good standing in the community and to become leaders in the frontier towns. They brought the eastern style of living with them and as Harvey Girls they had been trained to be good organizers. These women were usually the first to become involved in community activities and civic improvements. They fought for law and order and a better quality of life in the rough towns. Their voices were heard singing in the newly built churches and they organized social activities. The communities flourished because of their involvement.

The Harvey Girls were well respected, whether as a housewife or a waitress. People realized they were women of good character and it took a certain skill for them to serve a trainload of passengers in twenty-five minutes. Other waitresses might be looked down on, Harvey girls were not!

By the 1950s the era of the unified service provided by the Harvey Houses was a thing of the past, along with the classic railroad service itself. Individual Harvey House restaurants still operated but the Harvey Houses and the Harvey girls as a system had become a memory. The story of the Harvey Girls is an important chapter in the story of women, of the West, and of the growth of America. They were indeed a legend.

In Oklahoma, if your timing is right, you can still get a good sandwich at the Harvey House at the Hugo or the Waynoka train station. You can tour the dormitory, go through the Harvey House museum and even take a train. This is only available at certain times of the year so be sure and check the schedule. It is a wonderful nostalgic journey into the past.

RUBY DARBY

"The Toast of the Oil-Field Workers"

Ruby Darby added a new word to the English language. In oil rush days when a rig brought in a gusher someone might yell, "It's a Ruby Darby." Through time, the term was shortened to "It's a Darb" meaning it is something special.

Webster's dictionary defines "darb" as something superlative, with the origin from the astounding reputation of Ruby Darby, or as she was billed in theaters throughout the Southwest, "The Girl With The Blues."

A legend around the Oklahoma Oil Fields, Ruby Darby was indeed something special!

The speeding red car came down the dusty main street of the crowded oil boom town of Drumright at forty miles an hour. As expected, the already alerted local police stopped the speeder. From the back of the chauffeur driven car stepped a beautiful girl in a fur coat. Immediately, the news spread all over town: "Ruby Darby was in town and she wasn't wearing nothing under that fur coat."

This same scene was played out in all the major oil field towns across the state. By evening, more rumors would have circulated (most started by Ruby's own press agent), such as the local ladies society had protested the show and wanted it stopped. By curtain time, Ruby would have been bailed out of jail and the theater would be packed to the rafters.

And what a show it would be! As an entertainer

nobody could top her. She was a beautiful girl and her husky voice could bring tears to the eyes of the toughest oil-field worker. Ruby was said to be one of the first and possibly one of the greatest of the blues singers. Her trademark song which would always bring down the house was "Memphis Blues." Not only did her sultry voice captivate the audience but Ruby knew how to move her eyes, hips, and torso until she had every man in the audience under her spell. Everyone waited for the grand finale which would often be a strip tease.

Ruby was a popular adventurer and the legends of Ruby Darby traveled from oil field to oil field. It was said that Ruby "stripped at the drop of a driller's hat," that she had "danced bare skinned on a tool shack roof as men tossed silver dollars at her feet," and that she had "ridden a hoss completely nekkid down the mud and oil splashed streets of Kiefer." During one of her performances at a stag party in an oil-camp mess hall, Ruby created such a stir that a lamp was knocked over and the building went up in flames.

A popular saying of the day warned:

"If you've got a good man keep him home tonight, for Ruby Darby's in town and she's your daddy's delight."

It is difficult to know how many of the outrageous stories were true, or just rumors started by Ruby herself, who knew the wilder the stories the more packed the house would be for her performance. But Ruby had definitely found her niche, at a time when "Anything Goes" was the slogan for the wild oil field towns.

Oklahoma oil boom towns were noisy and crowded, wild and wooly, twenty-four hours a day, seven days a week. Drilling crews were mostly young men who worked hard and received very good wages. Without the stabilizing influence of family responsibilities, and with youthful exuberance, these young men sought recreation and en-

Ruby Darby in 1921. This photo and the photo on the back cover are courtesy of Frederick Graves, from pictures given to him by Ruby McEnery, Ruby's daughter.

tertainment when not on duty. Saloons, brothels, dance halls and gambling dens soon filled the towns. Towns quickly developed reputations and lived up to the notoriety.. There was Cromwell, called the "wickedest city in the United States." Kiefer was known as the toughest town east of Cripple Creek, Colorado. Whiz Bang was said to have gotten its name because it "whizzed all day and banged all night." However, the United States Post Office considered the name undignified and renamed the town DeNoya. Seminole had the area known as Bishop's Alley and nearby Bowlegs was home to scores of dance hall girls, bootleggers, gamblers and assorted criminals.

Like a breath of fresh air, Ruby Darby would suddenly appear in these towns and the most hardened of the oil field workers would turn soft at just the mention of her name. Ruby was their darling. She was a cut above the other entertainers. Not only did she put on an excellent show but it was obvious that she enjoyed herself and that she loved the workers as much as they loved her. Although many of the "Ruby Darby" stories were exaggerated, there were enough true stories to know that she was unpredictable, a gifted comedian, a truly great blues singer, and a free spirit with a great love for life. It was said that she was as "free as the Oklahoma breeze."

Ruby was a pioneer of the striptease, her fame preceding and rivaling Sally Rand. Burlesque shows at the turn of the century were not like the strip shows of today. If a woman just showed her ankle or shoulders during a dance, it was considered daring and risque. The shows were mostly a combination of several acts by singers, chorus girls and comedians. The best of the traveling shows was the Ruby Darby Show. Not only was this true in the boom towns, but also in the more sophisticated cities of Tulsa, Memphis, and Dallas, where Ruby's shows would play for more extended engagements at the better known theaters.

The half Cherokee entertainer was born in Alva, Oklahoma, shortly before the turn of the century. Her father was a former railroad detective and a local policeman. Ruby's show business career began about 1912 as singer with a blues band in Memphis, Tennessee. This in itself was quite unusual for a woman of the times.

By 1913, she was appearing at the Candy Land Theater in Dallas in the pony chorus, which was a chorus line of girls who were all the same size. Her big break came when she was picked from the chorus line by Ed Gardiner, the theater owner's son who not only promoted her shows, but subsequently married her. Ruby was only fifteen years old.

Ruby's show, *The Gal with the Blues* and her "Twelve Golden Gate Girls" hit the road about 1915, playing oil towns around North Texas and Oklahoma. Many of the other members of the troupe became her lifelong friends, including comedian and piano player, Hank Patterson and his show girl wife Daisy. Patterson later had many major television and motion picture roles, including Fred Ziffel, the owner of "Arnold the Pig" on television's *Green Acres*.

The success of the Ruby Darby show could be judged by the size of the show and the many elaborate costumes. Most similar shows boasted a maximum of eight chorus girls. The Darby show had sixteen. The Darby Girls had the most beautiful of costumes with several costume changes each show, and they always wore silk stockings.

A July 14, 1915, article from the Tulsa Daily World read:

> The Golden Gate Girls continue to make

the biggest kind of hit and the fact the program changes every day, presenting musical farce comedy of widely varying theme at each change and with attractive and distinctive wardrobe, gives the intending patron assurance of something different every time. Ruby Darby sings different topical songs each show but the crowds insist on the "Blues" time and time again.

A July 12, 1915, article from the Tulsa Democrat reported:

The Golden Gate Girls commenced a week engagement at the Wonderland yesterday and packed the house at every performance. The singing of Ruby Darby, "The Gal With the Blues," is a revelation. She practically stopped the show, for the audience insisted on repeat encores. With indescribable smoothness and an irresistible personality, Miss Darby scores a tremendous hit. It is safe to assert that no other tabloid musical comedy ever appearing at a local playhouse has ever met with such enthusiastic approval."

On August 12, 1914, the Tulsa Daily world reported:

Just three more days and the Ruby Darby show would leave for Atlanta, Georgia, and a tour of forty-two weeks over the entire southern vaudeville circuit."

Ruby was a modern day gypsy who refused to stay in one town too long. She would frequently leave one city in the middle of a successful run, simply because she wanted to move on to another place.

In the midst of her successful performances in Tulsa, a New York agent caught her show at the Broadway Theater. He talked her into coming to New York and auditioning at the Palace Theater, the mecca of big time vaudeville. She auditioned before two hundred of Broadway's toughest agents representing top vaudeville circuits. Their skeptical silence soon turned into cheering, similar to that of the oilfield roustabouts.

"The Girl With The Blues" walked from the stage into a longtime contract on the Keith-Albee circuit, with a starting salary of $750.00 per week that would have increased to $7500.00 per week within two years. Her first playing date was to be Baltimore, but she never arrived. Evidently, her independence and free spirit would not allow her to be tied down, and she returned to her beloved boom towns, where she could sing and dance and do what she wanted, with nobody else telling her what to do. Ruby had the talent to become a big time star but she couldn't stand the confinement.

Shortly after that, Ruby was divorced from Gardiner, who probably could not understand her rejection of the "big-time." She married an Oklahoma City banker, Luther Jones, but that marriage only lasted a year.

Ruby seemed to disappear for a while but later turned up in Los Angeles. She had married her third husband, a comedian named Bud Harrison, and had given birth to two children, Eugene and "Little" Ruby. The couple separated when "Little" Ruby was three and Gene was five years old. The children lived with their father but spent a great deal of time with their mother.

In 1977, a musical, *Girl With The Blues*, based on the career of Ruby Darby, was written and produced for the University of Tulsa by theater professor Frederick Graves.

Ruby's daughter, Ruby McEnery, attended the premier in Tulsa. In an interview with the *Tulsa Tribune*, "Little" Ruby described her mother as "a dear daredevil" and "a free spirit."

She said even while she was growing up, her mother was highly unpredictable. She might go to the store for a loaf of bread and end up in Mexico. But her warmth and love of life gave her family some wonderful memories.

In 1936, Ruby died of pneumonia, at the early age of 38 or 40. The disease was probably aggravated by alcoholism. She was still a popular entertainer, and just a few years previous to her death, had enjoyed a reunion with her old friends from the oil field days, Hank and Daisy Patterson. They had sat at the piano, sung some old songs, cried together, and relived memories of a day gone by.

Even today, oldtimers' eyes will light up with excitement at the mention of Ruby Darby's name. She was a legend, she was a star, she was a free spirit, but most of all, she was a DARB!

LYDE ROBERTS MARLAND

Oklahoma's Lady of Mystery

Oklahoma's most mysterious lady was Lydie (usually known as Lyde) Marland, the niece, adopted daughter, and wife of wealthy oil man and Oklahoma Governor E. W. Marland. Her life ran the gamut from being very poor to being very wealthy, from being in the forefront of the social scene to being a missing person for twenty-two years, and from being a lonely recluse to being an outspoken promoter who helped turn the Marland mansion into a museum.

In the very early evenings just before dusk, the residents of Ponca City were accustomed to seeing a shadowy figure stroll the streets. On closer inspection it was a woman wearing a long black dress over black and green checked pants, faded tennis shoes, a dark hat, and an old scarf. The small body was stooped forward staring at the street in front of her, not speaking to any one who passed by. She did not seem to notice the small boys playing ball or families out for an evening stroll. The people of Ponca City respected her privacy and her desire to be left alone. Still their hearts went out to her. They remembered another time when Lyde Marland had reigned supreme over Ponca City and when she was the first lady of the State of Oklahoma. Many remembered her as "Princess Lyde."

It was an exciting but frightening day in 1912 for the ten year old Lyde Roberts. She and her twelve year old brother George were on their uncle E. W. Marland's private railroad car on their way across the country to Oklahoma. Born in Flourtown, Pennsylvania, the children had never known any life but that of dire poverty. But like in a dream their mother's wealthy sister, Mary Virginia Collins Marland, and her husband, E. W., had offered to raise Lyde and George to relieve the financial burden of the Roberts family.

E. W. was a fantastically successful wildcatter who had made and lost one fortune in the Pennsylvania oil fields before moving to Oklahoma. There he had struck it rich in Ponca City where he developed the Marland Oil Company. In spite of their wealth, E. W. and Virginia's biggest disappointment in life was that in fifteen years of marriage they had not been able to have children. Now, their life was complete as they formally adopted Lyde and George and brought them to Oklahoma to raise as their own children.

The children soon found themselves living a life of luxury they did not know even existed. The Marlands lived in a beautiful home and entertained extravagantly. The children were given their own rooms, beautiful clothes, and expensive toys. They vacationed on Marland's magnificent yacht "Whitemarsh" and traveled in his private railroad car. They visited foreign countries, living the life of the oil rich. They played polo, rode horseback, and swam in their own private pool. Lyde attended fashionable schools in Long Island, New York and St. Louis, Missouri.

E. W. was considered the beloved benefactor of Ponca City. A generous man, he believed that success should be shared with the employees who helped make it possible. One-third of the population of Ponca City worked for him, and his good fortune affected the entire town. He financed houses for his employees and provided free social services. He gave lavishly to all the city organizations and landscaped the city streets with exotic shrubs. His home had the first indoor swimming pool in the state which was made available to his employees and he built a golf course which he opened free to the public. He also introduced polo and fox hunting to the prairie town.

Generous to the public he was even more giving to his family, but at the same time he was also a strict parent. In this atmosphere, Lyde grew to be a beautiful woman but extremely shy with a limited personal life.

In 1926, E. W.'s wife, Lyde's Aunt Virginia, who had been an invalid for many years, died. E. W. and Lyde turned to each other for comfort and one day realized their feelings of consolation and familial love had turned to romantic feelings. Two years after Virginia's death, in July of 1928, E. W. quietly had the courts annul Lyde's adoption and the couple boarded a train to Flourtown, Pennsylvania, where they were married in the home of Lyde's natural parents. Called the "scandal that shocked the Nation," newspaper tabloids from coast to coast jumped on the story of the marriage of the 54 year old millionaire to the beautiful 28 year old young woman who had been his adopted daughter for the last twelve years.

E. W.'s love for Lyde was so strong that he ignored the gossip and began building a $2.5 million dollar mansion for her. The magnificent Italian villa had 55 rooms, 15 baths, and three complete kitchens. Florentine murals decked the walls, Waterford crystal chandeliers hung in the dining room and ballroom, and the ceilings were Chinese Chippendale. The grounds contained three lakes, a polo field, an enormous swimming pool and lavish Hampton Court gardens. Prominent in the foyer was a portrait of Lydie as Carmen and in the garden was a sculpture of Marland's beautiful young wife.

The couple's happiness was cut short less than two years after they moved into the mansion when E. W. lost his fortune to the "Wolves of Wall Street." E. W. had borrowed money from J. P. Morgan, and when the debts could not be paid, Morgan's company, Continental Oil, took control of Marland Oil Company. E. W. was so broke that he even had to borrow money from fellow townsman and rival oilman Lew Wentz to complete his greatest legacy to the state of Oklahoma, the Pioneer Woman Statue, dedicated April 22, 1930.

Although the Marlands were down financially, they were not whipped. Holding their heads high they moved into the gardener's cottage on the vast estate. Actually, Lyde was not that unhappy. Very shy, she disliked being the mistress of the "Palace on the Prairie," as the villa had been nicknamed.

E. W. entered politics and was elected Oklahoma's tenth governor in 1934. As the youngest first lady in the history of Oklahoma, Lyde did not participate in many social functions. Never happy in crowds, the role of first lady was an ordeal for Lyde. She barely spoke at state dinners and avoided as many occasions as possible. She was very beautiful, slender (5'4", 107 lbs.) with huge brown eyes that were described as reminiscent of the eyes of a doe. And Lyde was as frightened as a doe. Her beauty and her shyness gave the impression to some that she was conceited and she became known as "Princess Lyde."

Following his term as Governor the couple moved back to the cottage on the grounds of the mansion. Marland had sold the mansion to the Carmelite Fathers, retaining the cottage and a small plot of ground. E. W. died in 1941. Lyde never seemed to recover from E. W.'s death and kept to herself in the cottage socializing very little.

Lyde had loved E. W. very much and resented the way, she felt, he had been treated by the very people he had dedicated his life to helping. If he had not been so generous with his money perhaps he would not have lost his oil company. Although he was governor at a very difficult time, during the Great Depression, he had instituted many programs which benefitted the people in the state. He had been a good governor, yet the people did not see fit to elect him Senator in 1936 or 1938 when he ran for the office. (Lyde would be pleased to know that historians of today regard E. W. Marland as one of the best Oklahoma Governors.) Lyde had always shied away from attention but E. W. had enjoyed being in the spotlight. For his sake Lyde had tried to socialize, but now that he was gone she did feel the necessity of putting on a false pretense.

Mysteriously, in March of 1953, Lyde loaded her green 1949 Studebaker with clothes and valuable paintings worth $10,000 and left Ponca City. Her last act was to take the beautiful statue of herself to a local monument company and order it smashed. She had lived in seclusion for so long that it was a while before anyone realized she was gone. Her brother George hired detectives and a massive search for Lydie was begun. But she had left no clues and in 1955, the Ponca City police officially listed Lydie Marland as a missing person.

No one heard from Lydie for many years except once each year, the Kay County tax assessor would receive an envelope containing the taxes on the small piece of property she still owned. It was always a little bit too much and the tax collector kept the surplus in a little box, just in case she ever showed up again. The envelopes would be mailed from various post offices across the country.

Lyde Roberts Marland. A 1976 photo of the original statue which stood north of the mansion. Discovered in 1990 and restored, it can be seen at the Marland Mansion. Courtesy of the Marland Estate.

From time to time people would report spotting Lyde somewhere. Someone claimed to have seen her at a supermarket in Arkansas City, Kansas, and said she fled when they called her by name. Someone else spotted her in Kansas City. George's detectives would follow each lead to no avail. Shortly before she was to be declared legally dead, Oklahoma investigators decided there was enough evidence to believe her still alive. The case was closed in December 1959.

Lydie's disappearance was almost forgotten when on November 22, 1958, an article appeared in the *Saturday Evening Post* entitled, "Where is Lyde Marland?" The article made claims of a lurid affair, beginning in 1950, between Lyde and Ponca City meter reader, Louis Cassel. The article showed pictures of the couple and said Lydie had given Cassel quite a bit of money to buy a farm but he had instead taken off for Seattle, Washington. Lydie was fifty-five years old at the time and according to the article was devastated by Cassel's disappearance and a few weeks after he left she packed her bags and disappeared. The article also showed a picture of a woman claiming to be the illegitimate daughter of Lyde and E. W. Marland, born before their marriage. (This was later proved to be untrue). Cassel was so incensed over the article that he sued the *Post*, but the outcome of the suit was never revealed.

There were other articles from time to time. Some claimed she was at a drug and alcohol rehabilitation center in Kansas City. At least one magazine claimed that her Aunt Virginia had died of drug and alcohol abuse.

No one actually knows where Lyde was during her twenty-two year disappearance. Just as suddenly as she had left, Lyde reappeared back up at the cottage at the mansion. She was seventy-five years old, a destitute and lonely woman. She lived on an annuity paid monthly by Conoco to her as the widow of the former chairman of the board of the company. Lyde never failed to write "thank you" on each check when it was endorsed. The mansion and the grounds had deteriorated. The religious order that had bought it filled in the swimming pool and eventually sold it to another order. That order was also unable to maintain the property .

Conoco, the company, that had taken over Marland's oil company now offered to put up half of the $2.5 million asking price if the city of Ponca City would come up with the rest and open the mansion to public tours. The city did not have the money or the desire to raise the funds, until Lyde broke her silence. In a letter to the editor of the local newspaper she wrote that she thought it was a good idea to restore and open the mansion to the public. The citizens of Ponca City voted a sales tax on themselves, and with the matching money from Conoco reopened the Marland Mansion. Lyde worked as an unpaid consultant with the restoration committee, showing them how the furniture had been arranged and explaining various features of the house. She was very anxious that the public enjoy the mansion and the grounds as they once were. Today, the Marland Mansions is one of the top tourist attractions in Oklahoma.

On occasion, visitors would see the stooped figure in black, always by herself, going in or out of the small cottage. Sometimes, when a musical event would be happening on the grounds at night, a dark shadow could be seen sitting on the hillside nodding her head to the music.

On July 25, 1987, Lyde Roberts Marland died of pneumonia in a Ponca City nursing home. Buried in Ponca City, only six people attended her funeral. The only flowers came from Conoco.

Later a memorial service was held at the mansion, which was attended by top officials at Conoco, Security bank (founded by Marland), city officials, and present and past members of the Marland Estate Commission. Lyde was described as "a proud, gracious and thoughtful lady."

In 1990, the statue of Lyde Marland was discovered where it had been buried for forty years. Lyde had ordered Glen Gilchrist from the memorial company to destroy the statue and had watched him smash the face. Gilchrist could not bear to see it destroyed and had buried the statue in back of his barn. After Lyde's death relatives of the deceased Gilchrist informed the mansion commission where it was buried. The statue was recovered and restored and now stands in the mansion's foyer. The only flaw is a crack that runs down the face like a tear. Perhaps it really is a tear for the tragic life of Lyde Roberts Marland.

Norma Smallwood, Miss America 1926. Courtesy of the Pioneer Woman Statue and Museum, Ponca City.

NORMA SMALLWOOD

Oklahoma's First Miss America

Oklahoma has a reputation as the Home of Beautiful Women including three Miss America's: Norma Smallwood in 1926, Jane Jayroe in 1967, and Susan Powell in 1981.

"The new Miss America, 1926, is Miss Tulsa, Oklahoma, Norma Des Cygne Smallwood." The announcer's words did not seem to faze Norma Smallwood. It took a moment for the news to sink in … she had actually been named Miss America, the most beautiful woman in the country.

Had it been a few years later Burt Parks would have broken into "Here She Is, Miss America," as the new winner of the most coveted crown in the country took her traditional walk down the runway at Atlantic City.

Television had just been invented in 1926, so the millions of would be viewers were denied the privilege of watching what has become an annual televised spectacular. Had they been watching, they would have been cheering for this classic beauty to represent America for the coming year.

This was only the fifth year for the Miss America pageant and the ceremony was described by some newspapers as indescribably corny. The King Neptune's Kingdom theme was carried out by the Master of Ceremonies, who was dressed as King Neptune. Norma was presented with a $5,000.00 golden statue of a mermaid, a $1,000.00 watch, and a "Many Dialed" radio. From her home town of Tulsa, she was presented with a $1,000.00 wardrobe from

Vandevers Department Store.

Norma's win was not a total surprise, as all week long, newspapers from all over the country had been predicting the crowning of the girl from Tulsa with the Grecian features and the buxom figure. A picture of her riding down the boardwalk in a rolling chair had been on the front page of newspapers around the world.

The beauty pageant had begun with 73 contestants and had been narrowed down to fifteen by the final night. Norma had won both the bathing suit and the evening gown competition.

The Miami Daily News, on the day following the pageant announced, "Unbobbed school girl wins Miss America," then asked the question, "Does this mark the beginning of the end for the flapper?" A Tulsa newspaper described her as having "Mona Lisa" looks and wearing her brunette hair "long as God and nature intended." Many newspapers described Norma as having a classic Grecian beauty with blue eyes and a severe coiffure of straight long chestnut hair worn in buns over her ears. They were most impressed with her buxom figure with measurements of 33-24-33, which was a contrast to the flat-chested era of the flappers. The new American ideal was eighteen years old, 5'4" and weighed 118 pounds. She was an art student from the Oklahoma College for Women in Chickasha and represented Tulsa in the pageant.

An astonished Norma sat in her hotel room the next day, reading the congratulatory telegrams from all over the world. With her was her mother and a representative from the Tulsa Tribune who served as her chaperon. A telegram from W. S. Skelly, President of the Tulsa Chamber of Commerce read, "Heartiest congratulations upon your individual success and the fame you have brought Tulsa." A telegram from Fox Pictures in Hollywood announced, "To: Norma Smallwood, Miss America... Can book for $1000 a week with Fox Pictures Inc." There were telegrams from the Governor of Oklahoma, the Mayor of Tulsa, her sponsor - *The Tulsa Tribune*, and several stage and screen offers. Within the next year, she would receive forty-three show business offers.

In an October 4, 1926, interview with *The Boardwalk Illustrated News*, Norma said, "All I am or ever hope to be I owe to my mother." The reporter said, "This aptly applies to Miss Smallwood and her mother, as the two are inseparable." In the years to come, this became even more apparent as Norma's mother was to play an important role in the events of her life.

Mahala Angela Smallwood was only sixteen when she married Edward Smallwood. At nineteen, she was left alone in Bristow, Oklahoma, with two small children, Lucille and Norma. Mahala became a cosmetician and later an oil and gas broker to support her family. She later married and divorced W. A. Dickerson. She was determined to raise and educate her children to the best of her ability.

Norma Des Cygne was a beautiful baby. Born May 12, 1909, she won her first beauty contest at the age of one when she was named Oklahoma's Most Perfect Baby in a contest in Bristow. Winning various beauty contest along the way, she attended school in Nevada, Missouri and Sherman, Texas, where she graduated from high school.

Her first year at the Oklahoma College For Women at Chickasha was very exciting, as she was chosen the most beautiful girl in school. Later that year, Rudolph Valentino named her the best dancer in a Charleston contest in Tulsa. As a sophomore, she won the Miss Tulsa and shortly thereafter, the Miss America Contest.

The next year was a whirlwind for Norma. Following the pageant she was honored at the Philadelphia Sesquicentennial Exposition.

On September 30 she arrived back in Tulsa, where she was welcomed by Governor M. E. Trapp, the Mayor and city council members, representatives of twenty-seven civic clubs, and twenty-five thousand Tulsans. It was the event of the year. A half-day holiday was declared by Mayor H. F. Newblock, and business men in suits, blue collar workers, housewives, and school children joined the civic organizations to march in the parade.

Although Norma said she preferred to go back to school, she would appear on stage for a year to earn enough money to further her training as an artist. She named her mother her manager and put her career in her hands. She joined the Keith-Orpheum vaudeville circuit where her name was flashed in lights across the nation.

At the end of her reign, Norma received some publicity of another kind. The Miss America pageant officials announced that Norma had walked out of the beauty pageant when the pageant officials refused to pay her the $12,000.00 she was accustomed to receiving for a personal appearance. A few days later Norma announced to the press that there had been a misunderstanding. Her manager had scheduled her for a personal appearance in Winston Salem, North Carolina, the evening of the pageant and she was unable to break the contract. She claimed she had notified the officials in advance that she would not be in attendance. For whatever reason, Norma was not there to place the crown on Miss Illinois, her successor as Miss America.

Norma returned to Oklahoma where she began dating the wealthy oilman Thomas Gilcrease. She still received many offers for the stage and motion pictures but it was clear that Mr. Gilcrease wanted her to remain in Tulsa. At the time she became Miss America, Norma was engaged to marry Pat Sublett, a school mate from Oklahoma City. The marriage was postponed and the relationship did not survive the instant fame and constant separations. She had other proposals but no one interested her until a casual meeting with Thomas Gilcrease at a Tulsa reception.

By the age of twenty-two, Tom was a self-made millionaire who had built a beautiful mansion overlooking Tulsa and was already becoming known for his art collections. When he met Norma he was thirty-eight, a divorced father of two sons and considered quite the catch of Tulsa. He was also soft-spoken, cultured, well read, and widely traveled. The young Norma was very impressed.

In a whirlwind courtship Thomas took Norma and her mother to Paris, France. He delighted in showing her the sights of all the important European cities. He showered her with affection, new clothes, and a $7,000.00 four and one-half carat diamond engagement ring.

On September 3, 1928, the couple was married quietly in the home of Judge S. Morton Rutherford, Jr., and honeymooned for a month at Thomas's Big Bear Lodge near Jackson Hole, Wyoming. They then moved into the Gilcrease home in Osage County overlooking Tulsa (the home is now the Tulsa County Historical Society and is on the property of the famed Gilcrease Museum.)

The eighteen year age difference did not seem to matter as the couple settled into the routine of married life. They were thrilled when a daughter Des Cygne L'Amour Gilcrease was born on June 12, 1929.

Troubles seem to begin after the birth of the baby when Tom wanted Norma to travel with him and she did not want to leave the baby. In October he persuaded her mother to drive his wife and baby to New York where they embarked for Europe. They took an elaborate apartment in Paris where Norma was exposed to a life of luxury she did not know existed. Three servants cared for the apartment and the family as well as a French nurse for baby Des Cygne. Norma and Tom would often leave the child in the care of her nurse and her grandmother for trips around Europe.

Tom would also be away from home frequently on business and Norma occupied her time by taking French and Spanish lessons. She also took lessons in art, history, and literature. She enjoyed the studies and also wanted to be worthy of Tom who was multilingual and well read. However, Tom was jealous and resentful of Norma's other interests and insisted she give up the lessons.

The couple returned to Tulsa in 1930 but the marital problems seemed to increase. Tom's business interest increasingly took him away from home and his young wife found the big house on the hill very lonely. They had social stature in the community, a beautiful home, but very little social life. To curb her loneliness, Norma turned one of the buildings on the estate into an art studio and spent long hours there by herself painting.

Finally, in 1933, Thomas Gilcrease filed for divorce and the biggest scandal in many years hit Tulsa. Tom alleged that for the first two years of their marriage they were happy, but that his mother-in-law Mahala Dickerson had moved into their home and alienated the affections of both Norma and his minor child. He claimed she had persuaded Norma to establish separate living quarters in their home and had encouraged her in refusing to eat or sleep with him.

The petition was unusually long and further alleged that during his absences from home on business trips, Norma and her mother entertained men in the home. He said he found cigar stubs, liquor bottles, and other evidence of disorderly parties. Tom had vowed at the age of six to never drink, smoke, or swear so he found these offenses disgusting. He also alleged that Mrs. Dickerson had established a beauty parlor in his home and that Norma had converted a garage apartment into a studio. Tom said that Norma was dominated by her mother, that she did not love him and wanted a divorce but that she was making enormous and unreasonable demands upon him for money and property settlements. He also filed for custody of their four year old child.

Details of a prenuptial contract emerged during the sensational divorce trial. It provided Norma with $1,000.00 cash at the time of her wedding and in case of divorce $5,000.00 a year for each year they were married. The contract even specified that the four and one-half carat diamond given to Norma upon their engagement was to be hers only as long as they were married.

A few weeks later Tom filed more accusations of Norma's excessive spending on clothing and jewelry. Then, in January, Norma filed an answer in which she denied all the accusations except that she had established an artist studio. She denied that her mother had undue influence on her and insisted that she had moved into the home at Tom's invitation. She insisted that rather than her mother, it was Tom who had driven away her affections by his constant criticism of her and her friends. She alleged that when she signed the prenuptial agreement, she was very young and naive and signed without the benefit of counsel or friends and without full knowledge of the contract. She asked she be granted a divorce and custody of their daughter.

The trial began on April 17, 1934, and lasted through May 2, 1934. Each day the courthouse was full of reporters and the curious. The case was long and drawn out with an excess of eighty-four witnesses called to testify.

When the fiery trial ended, the court found that Tom was not entitled to any judgement against Mahala Dickerson, but granted him a divorce on two grounds, extreme cruelty and gross neglect of duty. Norma was awarded $72,000.00, to be paid at the rate of $200.00 a month with the provision that she not remarry. She settled instead for a permanent allowance of $15,000 and later remarried.

They both appealed the decision to the Supreme Court of the State of Oklahoma, which in January of 1936 upheld the decision of the lower court. The Justice who wrote the opinion also gave custody of Des Cygne to her father. He wrote that in his opinion, both loved the child and the child would receive good treatment in either place but would be better cared for in the hands of her father.

In later years when some of the bitterness had diminished, Des Cygne spent time with both parents and was reported to have grown up with much love, admiration, and respect for both her mother and father.

Norma later married George Bruce, a Wichita oilman, and the couple made their home in Wichita with their one son. Norma's last personal appearance was in 1964 when she attended the opening of the Miss Oklahoma Pageant at Tulsa's Civic Center as a special guest and Oklahoma's only Miss America. Norma died at age 57 on May 8, 1966, just a few months before another Oklahoman captured the crown when Jane Jayroe was named Miss America on September 11, 1966.

Thomas Gilcrease did not ever marry again but instead put all his passions into collecting art and establishing what many consider the world's finest museum of art and history of the American West - The Thomas Gilcrease Institute of American History and Art.

Jane Phillips. Courtesy of Woolaroc Museum, Bartlesville, Oklahoma.

JANE PHILLIPS

"Aunt Jane"

Jane Phillips, as the wife of the fabulously wealthy oil man Frank Phillips, was equally at home as the gracious hostess to the upper crust members of society at a luncheon at the Plaza Hotel in New York City or at a back yard bar-b-que for the workers of Phillips Petroleum Company back home in Bartlesville. She was sophisticated and charming yet she was also compassionate and thoughtful. A woman of the world to many onlookers, yet back home she was thought of with affection as "Aunt Jane."

Jane lay back on the chaise lounge in her bedroom, kicked off her shoes, and reached for the ever present cigarettes on the table next to her. She had not realized how tired she was. It had been a wonderful party. She raised her glass of wine in a toast to her "Wall of Boyfriends," "To Frank and Jane, and a very happy fifty years together."

Jane was in her bedroom at Woolaroc, the country home or lodge just outside of Bartlesville, that Frank and Jane had built in 1926. The lodge, built as a retreat, had become quite a showplace and was the Phillips' favorite place to entertain. Jane's bedroom had especially become a place of curiosity as everyone wondered about her famed "wall of boyfriends." Over two hundred framed photographs of the men in Jane's life lined the walls. Not real boyfriends, as some unscrupulous gossips liked to intimidate, but men she knew and liked. Some were famous, others were just good friends. The pictures ranged from famous guests at Woolaroc like Wiley Post, Will Rogers, President Wilson, and Cardinal Spellman, to the ranch foreman and Jane's favorite chauffeur. The only criteria was to be liked by Jane. And if one of them came in disfavor, the photograph was immediately removed from the wall and placed in the discard pile.

Jane thought it had been a lovely party. As the music to "Let Me Call You Sweetheart" began, Frank took Jane into his arms to dance. "Betsy, you are as beautiful now as you were fifty years ago," Frank whispered to Jane.

All the guests were given a sneak preview of the new Woolaroc museum. Frank drove Jane up to the museum in a horse and buggy just like the one they had used on their wedding day in Creston. The museum was filled with thousands of roses and gladiolas, Jane's favorite flowers. Jane presented Frank with her anniversary gift, a bronze statue of himself created by Bryant Baker, the artist who had created the Pioneer Woman Statue in Ponca City.

Jane reached for her diary and entered the words, "I have truly had 50 golden years and am satisfied with my husband and children. They are all pure gold."

It was February 18, 1946, but Jane's thoughts went back to those days fifty years ago, when Jane Gibson was the " Belle of Creston, Iowa." The only daughter of a well-to-do banker, John Gibson and his wife Tilly, Jane was very popular and had many suitors. However, it soon became apparent the many boyfriends had been narrowed down to one - the new barber, who had started with one barber shop and in a short time owned all three shops in town. Although impressed with the enterprising Frank Phillips, a barber was not who John Gibson would have chosen for the darling daughter he called Betsy. But he knew Frank was ambitious and very much in love with his daughter, so he gave his blessing to their engagement.

Frank and Jane were married in a double wedding ceremony along with her brother Josiah and Marcelena Miller. Jane was beautiful in a light sage green brocade dress trimmed in silk and velvet. After the ceremony, the families went to the Gibson home for a wedding supper where Jane's father gave them $20,000 as a wedding gift.

The young couple moved into the Gibson home where Frank began working with Jane's father. He had promised to try banking, but he kept his barber shops, until he proved his worth. He did not want it said that he was successful because he married the banker's daughter. Frank found he enjoyed banking and it became a part of his life from then on.

In December 1898, Frank and Jane's joy was complete with the birth of their son, John Gibson Phillips.

Then in 1903 Frank became interested in a new venture that was to change their life forever - oil exploration in northeast Oklahoma. After convincing his father-in-law of the vast possibilities in oil investments, in 1904 Frank sold his barber shops and home in Creston and moved his family to Bartlesville, Indian Territory. He and his brother L. E. opened the Citizens Bank and Trust Company in Bartlesville and began their first wildcat drilling venture, the Holland No. I.

Jane would never forget her first day in Bartlesville. She and six year old John Philip were met at the train station by Frank who took them to rooms he had rented at the Almeda Hotel. There on the hotel lobby floor was a dead cowhand shot in an altercation just moments before their arrival. Jane went outside to get a breath of air, but the air was coated with the smell of oil. She took another look at the dusty streets and almost decided to take the next train back to Creston. But her devotion to Frank, and her belief that she should be by his side, made her reenter the hotel and begin unpacking.

After drilling three dry holes and with barely enough cash to keep drilling, Jane's prayers were answered when on September 6, 1905, Frank and L. E. hit a gusher in the Anna Anderson No. 1. Jane would never forget Frank's excitement. It made the hardships of the last few months all worth while. The well began producing 250 barrels of oil a day and in a short time they had more than eighty consecutive producing wells.

Frank and Jane, who had long since moved from the hotel, decided the time had come to build a finer house. Construction was begun and the family moved into their beautiful new Greek Revival style residence in 1909. The four story mansion with servants' quarters, gardener's cottage, and gazebo soon became the talk of the town. There was a ballroom on the third floor and a large circle drive to handle the carriages and automobiles for the many guests the Phillips entertained. It was extravagant but it was also homey, as no matter how wealthy they became, the Phillips remained best known for being down to earth people. They might travel all over the world and entertain royalty but the best times were around the grand piano in that home on Cherokee Street.

The Town House, as it was later to be called, was the first mansion in the new state of Oklahoma to be built by oil money. But it was no means the most extravagant. This was the time of huge fortunes being made from oil. Men willing to take a risk suddenly found themselves oil barons — Men like by Bill Skelly, Josh Cosden, H.V. Foster. Harry Sinclair, George and J. P. Getty, and E.W. Marland. The Skelly home in Tulsa became a show home, later to be overshadowed by Waite Philip's Villa Philbrook, the Marland Mansion in Ponca City, and the Buttran mansion in Oklahoma City, all built by oil men.

The next few years were a whirlwind, with parties, trips to Europe and Hawaii, around the world cruises, a penthouse in New York, and entertaining Presidents, Chiefs of State, and old friends like Will Rogers.

It was an exciting life but Jane enjoyed her times in Bartlesville just as much, with whist and bridge games, socializing and gossiping with friends, piano recitals and school events. Although Frank did not approve of his wife sewing, Jane took great pleasure in her needlepoint. The house was renovated in 1917, and in 1931 a $500,000 renovation was undertaken under the guidance of the famous architect Edward Buehler Delk, who designed the Country Club Plaza and the Philbrook mansion.

Jane's wall of boyfriends. Courtesy of Woolaroc Museum, Bartlesville, Oklahoma.

The Phillips were thrilled when in 1918 they became the legal guardians of two sisters just three and five years old. Always regretting they could not have more children themselves, the girls, whose names were changed to Mary Frank Phillips and Sarah Jane Phillips, soon became true members of the family.

The people of Bartlesville always felt as if they also were a part of the Phillips family. The nicknames "Aunt Jane" and "Uncle Frank" were truly affectionate. As the company grew, it seemed like every family in town had at least one member who worked for Phillips Petroleum Company. Frank was considered a fair and considerate employer. Jane was so well liked that the female employees began the Jane Phillips Sorority, which spread to other Phillips branches across the United States. At Christmas, Uncle Frank would be seen downtown handing out silver dollars to the children. And when a circus came to town, Uncle Frank bought every child in town a ticket.

The love for Frank was most expressed with the celebration of the 66th birthday of Mr. Phillips. The whole state had joined in the celebration. Visitors arriving by train as early as 4:00 a.m. were met and served breakfast by ladies of the Jane Phillips Sorority, and given tours of the Phillips Petroleum Company in town and the beautiful Frank Phillips Ranch and museum at Woolaroc. An air show featured sixty-six aerial bomb salutes and the words "FP," "66," and "Happy Birthday" were scrawled across the sky. Frank and Jane, along with Governor and Mrs. Leon Phillips, had driven the entire parade route waving and saying "howdy" to the thousands of people who lined the streets. The car they had ridden in was the $25,000.00 Chrysler specially built for King George and Queen Elizabeth of

England when they came to New York for the World's Fair. As Frank and Jane entered the reviewing stand the parade began. And what a parade! There were sixty-six units divided into three sections, each section to tell a sequence of Frank's life. Marching were Osage Indians in tribal dress, the Boy Scouts, pep squads, drill teams, civic organizations, and children dressed in circus costumes.

When the parade was over, Frank and the many guests attended a program at the Municipal Stadium where, after musical performances and many speeches, a twelve foot tall birthday cake in the shape of the Phillips office building was wheeled onto the stage.

That evening Uncle Frank and Jane managed to appear, at least for a few minutes, at each of the many cocktail parties, open houses, picnics, street dances and formal balls held all over the city in Frank's honor. Outside, the night sky was filled with rockets and explosions, including sixty-six varieties of fireworks and a brilliant "Happy Birthday" and a Phillips 66 shield. The dancing and the partying went on until the wee hours of the morning. In fact, Frank and Jane had put their guests on the 6:00 a.m. train back home to Missouri, Kansas, and Texas, before finally retiring at the ranch at Woolaroc.

There were many happy occasions to celebrate: the excitement of each new company venture - the development of the Phillips 66 logo, the service stations, the development of natural gas.

They were both so proud of their ranch "Woolaroc," which meant woods, air, and rocks. There, they entertained other oil field personalities, actors, actresses, wall street executives, religious leaders, politicians. There also, Frank's annual Cow Thieves and Outlaw Reunions began. Old time outlaws, real cowboys, Indians, and peace officers forgot their differences for a once a year celebration of buffalo meat and old time roping and riding.

But the celebrations, the travel, the mixing with celebrities, or the things money could buy, did not diminish the heartaches that were always present. They suffered through the deaths of their parents, of the baby Frank Phillips II, a twin of Robert, who died two days after birth, of Wiley Post, Will Rogers and many other good friends. The heartache of son John's lifelong fight with alcoholism, along with the embarrassment of some of his drunken escapades. Jane also lived with constant rumors of Frank's indiscretions. She felt that was a sign of the times and certainly not unheard of in the nouveau rich oil society. Jane knew the only mistress that was a true competition was "Madam Oil". Until Fern Butler. The romance that lasted for twenty two years.

Fern Butler was the first female employee hired by Phillips Petroleum in the early 1920s as the switchboard operator and Frank's secretary. Three years later, when the New York office was opened,

Phillips Home in Bartlesville.

Fern became the New York office manager.

Fern was beautiful with light brown hair, blue eyes and a stunning figure. She was also intelligent, hardworking, and extremely loyal to Phillips Petroleum and Frank Phillips. Fiercely independent, she loved the hustle and bustle of New York, going to the stock exchange and supervising a sizeable staff including three secretaries of her own. Career minded, she was happy being single and had no home wrecking intentions.

In fact, Jane and Fern genuinely liked each other. They exchanged holiday greetings and gifts and even traveled together. Fern adored the Philip's foster daughters and the family often vacationed at her fashionable Connecticut estate.

No one could remember exactly when the relationship changed.

As the business grew, Frank began spending more time in New York. Although they kept a suite at the Ambassador, Jane's responsibilities with the children, her circle of friends, and social and philanthropic obligations often kept her home in Bartlesville. After business hours, Frank and Fern often continued their conversations at dinner at the Plaza or the Stork Club, Fern's apartment, or weekends spent together at her Connecticut mansion. They enjoyed horseback riding together, going to the theater, and most of all, talking about the business world. Fern always knew Frank would never leave Jane and she did not want to destroy their marriage. She was not a gold-digger or a home-wrecker but she was deeply in love with Frank Phillips.

Although Jane had her suspicions, she never spoke of the affair except to her most trusted confidants. It was not until 1939, that Jane felt it necessary to put a stop to the romance. Gossip around

Bartlesville among both their friends and the business had become unbearable. The rumors were probably intensified by another woman who wanted Fern's job. But Jane could no longer ignore the situation; she had to take a stand.

When Frank admitted the affair had been going on for several years, Jane's response was cool, "Frank, these kinds of things are bound to happen. I can understand that. But Fern will have to go."

Fern was immediately fired, and true to his word, Frank ended the affair. The friendship continued until Frank's death many years afterward, but it was just occasional letters or phone calls between friends of many years.

Now back in her bedroom at Woolaroc, Jane read again the words she had just written in her diary. Yes, there had been problems, but what marriage of fifty years had not had problems. But the joys far overshadowed the sorrows. She would not trade the last fifty years with anyone. They had, indeed, been pure gold.

Just two years after celebrating their 50th anniversary, Jane Phillips died on August 1, 1948. Her body laid in state at the townhouse in Bartlesville where thousands of town people and friends from around the world came to pay their last visit to Aunt Jane. Frank died August 23, 1950, in Atlantic City, New Jersey. They are both buried at their beloved Woolaroc.

The town house, the ranch at Woolaroc, and the Woolaroc museum are open to visitors where the legacy of Aunt Jane and Uncle Frank continues.

OKLAHOMA'S FIVE INDIAN BALLERINAS

Yvonne Chouteau, Rosella Hightower, Moscelyne Larkin, Maria Tallchief and Marjorie Tallchief

An American Indian legend says that dance is the breath of life made visible. This legend was never more true than on November 17, 1991, when a mural was unveiled at the Oklahoma State Capitol depicting Oklahoma's five ballerinas who are all world-renown and who were all of Native American ancestry.

FLIGHT OF SPIRIT

It was standing room only at the State Capitol for the dedication of the historic mural entitled "Flight of Spirit." All five Oklahoma ballerinas, now retired from the stage, were present. This occasion also marked the first time they had ever appeared together. They had a wonderful time signing autographs and sharing reminiscences.

All five dancers were pleased with the mural that was commissioned by the State Arts Council of Oklahoma and painted by Mike Larsen, a Chickasha artist from Oklahoma City. They agreed with Mike's use of symbolism to depict not only their accomplishments in dance, but also their rich Oklahoma heritage. The mural portrays the dancers, symbolically, as five figures in white ballet dress. In the background is the "Trail of Tears," with the people's faces turned from their homeland toward the setting sun, which was Oklahoma. The five geese in the sky symbolized the free spirits of the five dancers.

The people in the middle represented the heritage of each dancer; Yvonne is Cherokee, Rosella is

Artist Mike Larsen, Yvonne Choteau, Rosella Hightower, Marie Tallchief, Majorie Talichief, Moscelyne Larkin, and State Arts Council Executive Director Betty Price pose in front of mural, Flight of Spirit. November 17, 1991. Courtesy of State Arts Council of Oklahoma.

Choctaw, Maria and Marjorie are Osage, and Moscelyne is Shawnee, Peoria.

The three pow wow dancers on the right depicted the ballerinas being taken to pow wow dances when very young, which influenced their dancing later.

Several young girls in the painting illustrated the young ages at which the dancers began dancing. Mike explained that the young girls also represented the dancers of the future.

Later, at a press conference, all five expressed their delight in being honored and their pleasure in the pride in the arts shown by Oklahomans.

The honorees admitted they regretted never having danced together. Two opportunities had been available but unfortunately the five could never be assembled in one place at one time. In 1956, they were honored with an Indian Ballerina Festival in Tulsa, but Marjorie was performing in Paris and could not attend. Then in 1967, a reunion performance was presented in Tulsa and Oklahoma City but Maria had retired and was unable to participate. The ballet entitled *The Four Moons* was composed by Louis Ballard with each ballerina performing her own choreographed dance. The music was performed by the Tulsa and Oklahoma City Symphonies. The cover was Indian artist Jerome Tyger's last work of art before his untimely death.

In 1982, the same four who danced in *The Four Moons*, Yvonne Chouteau, Rosella Hightower, Moscelyne Larkin and Marjorie Tallchief attended a special performance of *The Four Moons* by the Tulsa Ballet Theater in honor of Oklahoma's Diamond Jubilee. At the same time they attended the unveiling of a statue entitled *The American Indian Ballerina* at the Williams Center Garden, in Tulsa.

The ballerinas all agreed their Indian heritage

contributed to their success. They believe Indian dancers possess a lightness of foot, a sense of rhythm, and tend to be more spiritual. The Native Americans dance as a way of thanksgiving, celebrating, and mourning.

All over the world, people have been amazed that Oklahoma produced five world famous ballerinas, but each has achieved fame on her own and each has her own story.

YVONNE CHOUTEAU

The youngest of the ballerinas, Yvonne was also the youngest American ever (at the age of fourteen) to become a member of the Ballet Russe de Monte Carlo. Yvonne was born in Vinita and moved to Oklahoma City while still a baby. She is the direct descendent of Oklahoma's first white settler, the French fur trader, Auguste Chouteau.

An only child, her father said when she was born, "My daughter will be either an opera singer or a dancer." His own love of the arts influenced her greatly, as he took her to pow wows and performances of opera stars, dancers, and musicians appearing in Oklahoma City. At the age of four she attended a performance of the Ballet Russe at the Overholser Opera House and knew, without a doubt, that was the life she wanted.

She began dancing at age two and in 1933, at four year of age, she represented Oklahoma Indian dancers on American Indian Day at the World's Fair in Chicago.

In 1941, her father took Yvonne and her mother to New York City so she could study ballet for the summer. Just twelve years old, Yvonne did not know she would not return to Oklahoma City. She went to a tryout for the School of American Ballet and was awarded a lifetime scholarship.

Her dad returned to Oklahoma and Yvonne and her mother remained in New York. Two years later, she attended an audition for the Ballet Russe de Monte Carlo. At fourteen, she became the youngest American ever to be accepted into the prestigious internationally known company. On her 16th birthday, she danced her first solo part, "Priere" in the ballet *Coppelia*. At age twenty-one, she was elevated to ballerina status and danced "Juliet" in *Romeo and Juliet,* which became her trademark dance.

In the 1950s, Yvonne met, danced with, fell in love with, and married Miguel Terekhov. In 1958, they left the Ballet Russe and toured North and South America as guest artists and lived in Uruguay for a few years. After the birth of two daughters, they decided to give up touring and return to the United States.

Yvonne and Miguel Terekhov became artists-in-residence at the University of Oklahoma and developed the school's dance department. They also organized and directed the Oklahoma City Civic Ballet for ten years.

At the age of eighteen, Yvonne became the youngest member elected to Oklahoma's Hall of Fame. She has been a goodwill ambassador for her state since childhood.

ROSELLA HIGHTOWER

A Choctaw, born on a pecan and cotton farm in Ardmore, Rosella showed a talent for dance at an early age. Recognizing her talent, her parents took her to Kansas City where she could study at the Dorothy Perkins School of Dance.

All of the ballerinas had a mentor or someone who encouraged and promoted their talents. For

Yvonne Chouteau, it was her father; for Moscelyne Larkin, it was her mother; and for the Tallchief sisters, it was their mother who was their strongest supporter. Dorothy Perkins was the great inspiration for Rosella.

Rosella joined the Ballet Russe de Monte Carlo in 1938, and in 1941 joined the Ballet Theater as soloist. She was noted for her emotionality and sensuality on stage.

In 1947, she left the United States to become the principal dancer with the Grand Ballet du Cuevas. When she appeared in Paris, she was an overnight sensation. She still remains the superb example of American ballet in Europe.

Rosella was known as a strong technician and an excellent choreographer. She was named artistic director of the Paris Opera Ballet in 1980. A noted teacher of dance, she left performing to become the director of the Center for Classical Dance in Cannes, France.

MOSCELYNE LARKIN

If ancestry plays a part in the making of a ballerina, then Moscelyne's heritage of a Russian dancer mother and part-Indian father gave her a head start. Her parent's romantic love story began when her mother, Eva Matlogova, newly in the United States, appeared, for one night, in Oklahoma City as a member of the Wilson Musical Comedy Company. R. L. Larkin, a young business student, attended the show and fell in love. He followed her on tour and they were married on stage after the performance in Joplin, Missouri. He then took her back to his home in Miami, Oklahoma.

Moscelyne was born in Miami and received her first dance lesson there from her mother, then later in Tulsa where Miss Eva became known as the finest dance teacher. Recognizing her daughter's talent, Eva took her to New York City for further training.

At fifteen, Moscelyne became a member of the Original Ballet Russe, dancing first as a soloist, then as ballerina, all over Europe, South America, and the United States from 1941 to 1947.

She was known for her tiny physique, sparkling personality, and tremendous jumps.

In South America, in 1944, Moscelyne was married to Roman Jasinski, ballet master and first dancer with the company. As first dancer and ballerina, the husband and wife team joined the Ballet Russe de Monte Carlo in 1948. In 1954, their son Roman was born. One of the highlights of her life was dancing in *Swan Lake*, "having a wonderful secret from the audience - that I was pregnant."

Wanting more family life, the Jasinskis left New York in 1956 to found the Tulsa Civic Ballet and School, now the Tulsa Ballet Theater, the state's oldest ballet company. Moscelyne and Roman served as Artistic Directors, until Roman's death in 1991. As Artistic Director Emerita, another highlight in Moscelyne's life was when her son, a well known dancer, was appointed Artistic Director of the Tulsa Ballet Theater.

MARIA TALLCHIEF

Born in the small town of Fairfax, Oklahoma, Maria always remembered her first dancing lessons. They were at the Broadmore Hotel in Colorado Springs when Maria was only about four years old. After that, a teacher came to Fairfax from Tulsa, once a week, to teach her and her sister Marjorie ballet. They also had piano lessons.

In an interview with the Oklahoma Historical Society in 1972, when she was inducted into the Oklahoma Hall of Fame, Maria said she was always rather embarrassed. She was shy, but everyone seemed to think the Tallchief girls were child prodigies and wanted them to perform at rodeos or other town celebrations.

She said this was the era of Shirley Temple and the family was persuaded to move to California where there were "good teachers" and the girls would have a better chance of success.

Maria studied dance and piano and became proficient in both as well as a good student academically. Upon graduation from Beverly Hills High School, she went to New York and auditioned and was accepted for the Ballet Russe de Monte Carlo. She was just 17.

By the time she was twenty, she was first ballerina for the New York City Ballet. Maria would never forget being 20 years of age, standing on stage at the Paris Opera House with a whole symphony in front of her, and in the audience were the most eloquently dressed and sophisticated people in the world. She thought how just five years before, she had been studying her high school French thinking someday she might have a use for it.

Maria was married, for a time, to George Balanchine and helped him create the New York City Ballet, where she was its best known dancer at the time. In 1949, the audience watched in awe as she danced the leading role in the ballet *Firebird*. It was the first time in history that the New York City Ballet played to a full house and the critics adored Maria in *Firebird*.

As one of the most acclaimed American ballerinas, Maria had many memorable moments, such as dancing at the White House before President

Eisenhower, who presented her the Woman of the Year Award and named the day Maria Tallchief Day. She also was congratulated backstage by Queen Elizabeth, after a benefit performance for the Royal Ballet. In Russia, she was invited to supper with Premier Nikita Khrushchev. The little girl from Fairfax, Oklahoma had come a long way.

MARJORIE TALLCHIEF

Born in Fairfax, Oklahoma, Marjorie was always proud of her heritage. Her father, Alexander Tall Chief, was a fullblood Osage Indian. Her mother was of Irish, Scottish, and Dutch ancestry. The younger sister of Maria, her background was much the same, moving to California, studying dance and piano and graduating from Beverly Hills High School.

Marjorie joined the American Ballet Theater as a soloist in 1944 and danced as first soloist with the Original Ballet Russe from 1946 to 1947. In 1947, she was named a ballerina with the Grand Ballet du Marquis de Cuevas, an American ballet company based in Europe. There she created roles with her husband, the late George Skibine. Marjorie, as the premiere of the Paris Opera, was known as a lyric dancer with an extraordinary gift of interpretation. George Skibine was a young gifted dancer, choreographer, and director.

In 1957, the couple joined the permanent star roster of the Paris Opera Ballet. They were the first Americans (George by naturalization, Marjorie by birth) to join this prestigious company. The couple were considered by many as the most adored of the romantic pairs in the European theater.

In 1958, Marjorie became the first American ballerina since World War II to perform in the Bolshoi theater in Moscow. In 1961, she led the Paris Opera ballet gala performance at Versailles, in honor of the official visit of President and Mrs. Kennedy to France.

After retiring from the stage in 1966, she was instrumental in developing the Dallas Civic Ballet and establishing its nationally known school.

Following her husband's death in 1981, she joined her sister, Maria, in Chicago, serving as director of the Chicago School Ballet until 1989, when she was named the Director of Dance at the Harid Conservatory in Boca Raton, Florida. In 1991, she was named to the Oklahoma Hall of Fame.

Although retired from the stage, these five dancers continue to represent their native state with grace and charm bringing a recognition that Oklahoma is a land of talent, culture, and refinement.

COL. ROSEMARY HOGAN

"The Angel of Bataan"

One of the first woman heroes of World War II and one of the first nurses to be awarded a purple heart was Colonel Rosemary Hogan of Chattanooga, Oklahoma. She was known as the "Angel of Bataan" for her acts of courage and service to others while being held a prisoner of war by the Japanese.

Landing on the Philippine Islands in December of 1941, Rosemary Hogan smiled, "I think I could like this place." Little did she know that what should have been a routine pleasant duty in a beautiful tropical setting would instead turn into a nightmare.

For a small town Oklahoma girl, who had never been out of Oklahoma before becoming an army nurse, the whole world was an exciting new adventure. Now as she watched the waving palm trees, smelled the aroma of the tropical flowers, and walked on the sandy beaches, she thought the Philippine Islands must surely be the loveliest, most peaceful place in the world.

Certainly, it was quite different than Ahpeatone, Oklahoma, where she was born on March 13, 1912. Ahpeatone, in southwestern Oklahoma, was so small that she attended school in nearby Chattanooga, a big town of four hundred people, twenty-five miles southwest of Lawton. She was valedictorian of her class at Chattanooga and received a nursing scholarship given by local doctor George E. Kerr.

It was an exciting day for Rosemary when she arrived at Scott-White Hospital in Temple, Texas, to begin nurse's training. From the beginning, she knew that nursing was her calling and she excelled in her training. In 1936, Rosemary entered the Army Nurse Corps at Fort Sill and served at the post hospital before being sent to the Philippines in 1940.

She did not have long to enjoy her tropical holiday when the Japanese bombing of Pearl Harbor on December 7, 1941, shocked the world. Heavy fighting also broke out in the Philippines as World War II was declared. As disaster after disaster befell the American and Filipino forces, Nurse Hogan was sent to Bataan Peninsula to set up a 1000 bed hospital.

As chief army nurse, on December 24, 1941, she took twenty-five U.S. Army nurses and twenty-five Filipino nurses on their new assignment. That beautiful scenery, enjoyed only a few months previously, now became a frightening maze of jungle ready for an instant ambush. Rosemary wondered if the old Filipino busses camouflaged in brush would ever make it to Bataan. After a hard day of traveling, the group of tired hungry nurses finally arrived at the site of Hospital No. 1 at Limay.

The nurses were quite dismayed to find that the hospital was a hospital in name only. It was actually only a huge warehouse with all the hospital equipment packed for overseas shipment. Rosemary quickly organized her group to unpack, inventory the supplies, and set up medical stations. In short order, to the disbelief of all involved, a functioning hospital was established.

Needless to say, Christmas Day was not a day of merriment and cheer but one of total exhaustion.

Within a short time the hospital was ordered to move closer to the fighting, a little farther down the peninsula to what was called "Little Baguio". Col. Hogan served as the Assistant Chief of Nurses until she was wounded in April of 1942. Rosemary and another nurse were assisting an army surgeon in the operating room with bombs falling all around them. They stayed on duty as long as they could and finally hid outside in foxholes. She was badly injured, the army hospital at Bataan was destroyed, and Nurse Hogan and the other injured were taken to Corregidor to recover.

Col. Hogan was one of the first nurses in the Pacific Theater to be awarded the Purple Heart. The folks back home also celebrated as a 1942 Chattanooga newspaper clipping announced,

Col. Rosemary Hogan. Courtesy of Gladys Hyder, Rosemary's sister.

" The little southwestern Oklahoma village of Chattanooga, 326 residents strong, is thrilled to the account of Rosemary Hogan's fortitude on Bataan wherein, injured severely by shrapnel splinters, she lay uncomplaining so that dying soldiers would have access to the doctors."

"Relatives and friends here are still anxiously awaiting word that she is on the big island fortress of Corregidor. Miss Hogan was reported to have been removed from Bataan with several other nurses after Japanese destroyed the Army hospital where she was serving."

But tragedy was still to come, for as the nurses were being evacuated, their plane was forced to land on Mindanao Island and they were captured by the Japanese. Nurse Hogan was imprisoned at Santo Tomas prison in Manila, until the liberation by American forces in 1945.

Perhaps it was her strong Oklahoma heritage that sustained Rosemary during those three years of internment after the fall of the Philippines. She didn't take time to feel sorry for herself but plunged into caring for the wounded prisoners.

A letter written by a fellow officer said,

"During her internment, Col. Hogan performed nursing duties, helping to take care of the many U. S. and Allied prisoners held captive then. She displayed her usual courage in the face of adversity, helped cheer the discouraged, provided the nursing care possible with available supplies and equipment, and did everything necessary to alleviate the distress of fellow prisoners without regard to her personal comforts."

Liberation Day, February 4, 1945, was a great day for the prisoners. At first, the prisoners thought it was the Japanese coming for them so they feared the worst. When they realized it was the American

Army which meant freedom, their cheers and shouting rang throughout the camp.

Rosemary was surprised to find that one of her liberators was an old friend, Theo Tanner of Hollister. Theo and Rosemary had been acquainted during their teenage years. Imagine someone from home coming to the rescue! Rosemary did not take much time to celebrate, but continued at her job of mercy, tending to the sick and wounded.

After the war, a woman of lesser tenacity would have retired from the army and gone home to a more normal way of life. But the Air Force Nurse Corps was a new service and Rosemary was excited by the challenge of helping to establish it as a viable service. She served in many assignments, including Chief Nurse, Boling Air Force Hospital; Chief Nurse, Technical Training Air Force Base at Biloxi, Mississippi; and Chief Nurse of the Tactical Command, Langley Air Force Base, Virginia; from which position she retired.

A major breakthrough for women in the Army Air Force was when Rosemary Hogan was given the rank of Full Colonel. She was among the first four women officers to hold that rank.

Col. Hogan married Major Arnold Luciano, USAF, and after retirement they made their home in San Antonio, Texas. Upon her death on June 24, 1964, Col. Rosemary Hogan was buried at Arlington National Cemetery.

In 1977 a new dormitory at Sheppard Air Force Base at Wichita Falls was named in her honor.

Long after the war has ended, many American Veterans with misty eyes still talk of the "Angels of Bataan," the heroic army nurses who gave them the courage to withstand the horrors of the prison camp. And foremost is the name of Rosemary Hogan, Oklahoma's own "Angel of Bataan."

Fern on Ray's Model A Ford before he sold it for $65 to get married. Courtesy of daughter, Marquita Johnson.

FERN McFARLAND

"Granny Fern"

If you meet someone today who lived in Seminole, Oklahoma, or even salesmen who called in that area, just ask if they ever ate at "Granny Fern's Kitchen." Chances are, their faces will light up in remembrance of the best pie they ever ate and the extraordinary woman known as "Granny Fern."

Francis "Fern" Bottoms McFarland never forgot the first time she saw Ray McFarland. In fact, she always told her children and grandchildren, "He was the handsomest man I ever saw. Why, he was standing right in front of Park Drug Store in Seminole, dressed in a three piece suit, with his foot on the bumper of a new Model A Ford. He was leaning back, twirling a gold chain with his car keys that was attached to his belt. I thought he looked just like Rudolph Valentino."

At the same time Fern was making this appraisal, Ray was also looking Fern up and down. And he liked what he saw. As he later told his co-workers at Park Drugstore, "I just saw the most beautiful girl I ever saw in my life. I am going to ask her out for a date and if that works out, I just may marry her someday." Fern, who was still in high school and working as an apprentice hair stylist at a local beauty shop, soon found out that Ray was a clerk at the drug store. The next few days, she seemed to need some toiletry item each day. As Ray waited on her, she discovered that he had grown up in nearby Bowlegs, had come to Seminole in 1931 to work at the drug store, and was a pharmacy student at the University of Oklahoma in Norman.

Ray finally got up enough nerve to ask Fern to accompany him to the picture show, to see Claudette Colbert and Clark Gable in "It Happened One Night." Ray told Fern that a few years ago a young oil field worker had come into the drug store and wanted to buy some medicine but did not have any money. When Ray said he could not give any more credit to oil field workers, the young man said, "You just wait and remember my name - Clark Gable. Some day I will be famous". Ray was not sure but he thought the man was the same as the leading man in the film.

Fern knew the story was probably true. There were many rags to riches stories coming out of the oil field towns. Seminole was one of the most sensational oil cities in the state. Her parents and their friends talked often of how on July 20, 1927, a huge gusher had changed their town forever. Overnight, the town was full of speculators, producers, lease buyers, oil drillers, storekeepers, dance hall girls, swindlers, gunmen and riffraff from everywhere. Suddenly, Seminole had everything the most colorful frontier towns and most spectacular mining camps had and then some. Prohibition did not stop the many bootleggers who kept up with the demand for booze, and dance halls flourished around the area in the north end of town known as Bishops Alley.

The area was full of notorious criminals such as Pretty Boy Floyd and women with names like Barrel House Sue and Big Emma Smythe. In the ten years of Seminole's height of glory, there were 33 arrest for murder and 33 convictions. Had it not been for the town's strong law enforcement and the support of the many honest public spirited citizens, the town would have been much worse. Even so, it was as if every store clerk, telephone operator, truck driver and dance hall girl thought they would get rich; but only a few really did.

Fern had grown up living in a company oil town outside of Seminole. Her father was a roustabout for the Carter Oil Company which, as most of the oil companies did, maintained its own town for employees. The town had its own grocery store, gas station, school, and inexpensive homes that employees could rent or buy. In the center was the company building that contained offices and a recreational center. Everything the employees or their families could want was provided right on site.

Ray had grown up a few miles from Seminole in Bowlegs. Before the oil boom in 1927, Bowlegs was just a few homes and a post office in a general store owned and operated by Ray's parents. With the discovery of oil came gamblers, women, liquor peddlers, vultures, adventurers, and the toughs of all descriptions. In a few years, Bowlegs was widely publicized by newspapers as the "toughest town in the United States."

But by 1934, much of that early day frenzy had died down. Seminole was becoming more like a normal town when Ray and Fern began dating. They often attended the movies if they could scrape up fifteen cents each, but more often they would go to Fern's house to listen to George Burns and Gracie Allen or Fibber McGee and Molly on the radio. Or they would go on drives in Ray's most prized possession, his Model A Ford.

In June, when Fern graduated from Seminole High School, Ray began pressuring her to get married. Although Fern was deeply in love she refused, saying they did not have the money. Vowing she would only marry once, Fern had her heart set on a large formal wedding. She wanted to have the grandest wedding in Seminole, with a wedding dress and a reception with a real wedding cake. Finally, in desperation, Ray said, "What can I do to get you the kind of wedding you want?"

Fern thought for a moment. "Well," she said, "you could sell your car."

"But that is how I get to pharmacy school!" Ray exclaimed.

"You could ride the autobus. It goes back and forth from Seminole to Norman each day, and you just have two more years," came Fern's ready solution.

Sunday, September 22, 1934, was a beautiful Indian Summer day in Seminole. But the day was not as beautiful as Fern Bottoms, in her gorgeous long white satin wedding dress with the long train trailing behind, as she walked down the aisle of the First Baptist Church in Seminole. Her mother, who did not have a sewing machine, had lovingly stitched every seam on the dress by hand. On her head, Fern wore a circlet of flowers with a short veil. Years later, her daughters would play in that wedding dress, never fully appreciating the sacrifices it represented.

It was a real wedding, just like Fern always dreamed of having. Her best friend Lenore Haynes was the maid of honor and Ray's best man was his friend Doyan Cox. There were four bridesmaids, two flower girls and a ring bearer. The wedding cake was a work of art. The flower bedecked church was filled to capacity and indeed, all Seminole talked of the magnificent Bottoms-McFarland wedding.

True to his word, Ray sold the Model A. It was twelve years before the young couple could afford another car. For two years he rode the autobus to school each day. The autobus was a station wagon that carried eight passengers and left Seminole at six o'clock each morning and departed from the University in Norman at four each afternoon. Then Ray would go to the drug store to work the night shift. But he never regretted his decision. In later years, he would laugh and say it was the best decision he ever made. For their 50th wedding celebration, the cake was shaped like a Model A car.

Fern also worked hard at the beauty shop. The couple rented a one bedroom apartment above a store, and on hot evenings would pull their mattress out on the roof to sleep in the cool moonlight. They were in the midst of the depression but they did not notice. So what if they could only afford meat once a week, they could buy a peck of potatoes for fifteen cents, and five pounds of coffee for sixty cents. The most important thing was they had each other and they had a dream. The dream of someday owning their own drug store, and secretly, Fern also envisioned that one day she would own her own business.

That dream came true in 1946 when Ray and Arthur Christenson formed a partnership and bought the Sooner Drug Store. By this time, Ray and Fern had two daughters, Marquita Rae born Dec 27, 1939, and Melodie Beth born March 17, 1945. Fern also had her own business - a beauty shop she operated from her home.

The hard working, friendly young family became popular in Seminole, often listed among the outstanding citizens. They believed in supporting the community that treated them so well. Ray was President of the Bowlegs Alumni Association and the Seminole Chamber of Commerce. Fern was PTA President. At one point, when a school bond vote was in jeopardy, she organized a series of block coffees and a carpool to take voters to the polls. The bond passed overwhelmingly.

But it was as "Granny Fern" that Fern McFarland gained her fame and achieved the success that she dreamed of for so many years. In 1953, Ray and Fern bought the Central Drug Store and the whole family became involved in the operation.

Ray put in the finest pharmacy in the area and stocked all the latest toiletry items. He sold everything from hearing aids to air conditioners.

Fern put her creative talents to work and turned the old soda fountain into a thriving lunch counter with ten booths. Never afraid of work, she would rise at five o'clock each morning to bake fresh rolls, home made bread, and her delicious pies. She would be at the lunch counter each day serving her famous bar-b-que, spaghetti and sandwiches. After school, the girls would walk to the drug store to help out in the pharmacy or at the lunch counter.

"Granny Fern's" became famous, not only as the best place in the area to eat, but also for Fern's friendliness and lighthearted banter with the customers. Everyone knew it would never be boring at "Granny Fern's." They always left with a full stomach and a happy heart.

One day, Fern looked up and saw a handsome dark haired man, with a black mustache, looking at the belt buckles on the counter. "How much discount will you give me on this buckle?," the man asked.

"Why, I don't give discounts," Fern answered indignantly.

"But, I am Ernie Ford," replied the man.

"Pleased to meet you, I am Fern McFarland," Fern held out her hand.

"But you don't understand, I am known as Tennessee Ernie Ford."

"Well, folks around here know me as Granny Fern."

"Don't you listen to the radio? I'm on the radio every Friday night."

"Lord, Mister, I don't have time to listen to the radio. I'm baking bread every night."

At this, the tall stranger broke down with laughter. " This is wonderful," he exclaimed. "Have you ever heard of the song "Sixteen Tons?"

"Well, yes," Fern admitted. "My daughter Markie does listen to that song. You mean you are that Tennessee Ernie?"

"Let me buy both of us a piece of that coconut pie that keeps you so busy and let's sit a spell," laughed the famous singer who was in Seminole for a benefit performance. Ford was so captivated by the woman who did not recognize him, that he told the story many times after that, and for many years sent Fern a Christmas card.

In 1965, business had increased so much that the McFarlands bought a bigger building for the "new and improved" Ray's Central Drug Store, a dining room for Granny Fern's Kitchen, and another room for Fern's Dress Shop. That next year, "Granny Fern Day" was celebrated by The Lions Club and the Tuesday Lions Club Widows, that met for lunch at Granny Fern's every Tuesday for many years.

Fern McFarland was a marketing genius long before marketing degrees were available. She had a sense of knowing what her customers wanted, and devised clever ways to provide those wants.

In one of their first stores, she talked Ray into selling school books to bring traffic into the business.

A creative businesswoman, Fern knew how to study people. Her dress shop was successful because she knew Seminole women's tastes were not the same as Oklahoma City women. She also knew her products. When she wanted to add cosmetics to the drug store, she went to New York City for advice.

Granny Fern's Kitchen was known all over Oklahoma as serving excellent food in a homey atmosphere. She never skimped on ingredients. If a recipe called for a pound of butter, that is what she used, regardless of the cost. She sold the restaurant many years ago but people still talk about the best pie they ever ate - at Granny Fern's in Seminole, Oklahoma.

Ray and Fern celebrated their golden anniversary in 1984. They had semiretired and were enjoying traveling, their grandchildren, and spending the winters in Arizona, when Fern died on October 27, 1988. The editorial in the Seminole newspaper summed up Fern's life in Seminole this way:

"Fern opened what has become a Seminole area landmark, Granny Fern's Kitchen. We still have an occasional salesman call on us and ask about the restaurant that served the good spaghetti and great strawberry pie. Those were a couple of Fern's real winners.

They buried Fern Saturday. Seminole may of had a better retail businessperson but we sure don't know who it would be. We admired her aggressive business talents, we enjoyed her outspoken opinions, we appreciated her cheery upbeat outlook, we envied her energy and enthusiasm and we are honored to have known her and call her our friend. Fern will be missed by an awful lot of us."

What a wonderful way to be remembered by your townfolks!

Granny Fern's Strawberry Pie
Makes 2 pies

2 cups water
2 small boxes frozen sweetened strawberries
2 cups sugar
1 tablespoon less than 1/4 cup lemon juice
4 heaping tablespoons corn starch
red cake coloring
1 quart frozen strawberries

Mix dry things together, add to water, frozen stawberries and lemon juice. Bring to boil until it thickens. ... cool. Pour over fresh strawberries in cooked pie shell. If fresh strawberries are not available, pour over bananas. Top with a tad of whipped cream.

Fern also made this by putting a layer of bananas in the cooked pie shell before adding fresh strawberries.

Arizona Donnie Kate "Ma" Barker with husband George. Unpublished picture from the private colletion of Dee Cordry.

ARIZONA DONNIE "KATE" BARKER

The Infamous "Ma" Barker

In the late 1920s and early 1930s the United States seemed to be overrun with gangsters. The Federal Bureau of Investigation began publicizing a "most wanted" list . Among those listed were George "Machine Gun" Kelly, John Dillinger, "Baby Face" Nelson, Clyde Barrow and Bonnie Parker, Charles "Pretty Boy" Floyd, and Kate "Ma" Barker. Ma Barker made her home in Tulsa, where some people considered her just an overprotective mother of four mobster sons, but FBI Director J. Edgar Hoover described Ma Barker as "a cold-blooded creature of evil."

"My boys are good boys; they always go to church with me on Sunday," was the way Ma Barker dismissed the neighborhood complaints against her four boys. Around Webb City, Missouri, where the boys grew up, they were known as malicious troublemakers, but to Ma they were just mischievous youngsters. This became a way of life, with Ma always forgiving the boys for whatever transgressions they might be involved in. The boys, knowing that no matter what kind of trouble they got in, Ma was always there to defend them.

Ma was born Arizona Donnie Clark in 1871 to poor farmers in Missouri. She always hated her name and began calling herself Kate. In 1892, she married a farmer and miner from Lebanon, Missouri. To this union was born four sons, Herman, Lloyd, Arthur (nicknamed Doc) and Fred. When the boys were small, the family moved to Webb City where George worked at the zinc mine.

It was in Webb City that Kate was nicknamed "Ma," a name that would stay with her for the rest of her life.

Growing up in Missouri, Kate had heard stories of the legendary Jesse James. She thought he was a great hero and dreamed of living such an exciting life as the James Boys. She soon found that life with George was not very exciting. She made up for the boredom in her life by doting on her four boys. The boys grew up knowing that Ma ruled the household and as far as she was concerned her boys could do no wrong. No neighbor, police chief, or minister could ever convince her otherwise, although many tried.

The family had few friends, in Webb City, because of the reputation of the Barker Boys. Ma had one good friend from church but their relationship ended over a feud between their sons.

In 1910, after Ma got Herman off from a charge of highway robbery, she left George and with the boys moved to Tulsa. They moved into a small frame house at 401 N. Cincinnati. The house soon became the headquarters for a gang of teen age "punks" known as the Central Park Gang.

George joined his family for a short time but found he did not have any influence on his family and could not put to a stop to their criminal activities. The house on Cincinnati Avenue outgrew its reputation as a clubhouse for teenagers and became a full fledged hideout for escaped convicts and bank robbers on the run. The boys were becoming more involved in what was to become their lifelong career of crime.

Perhaps, this is when Ma became known as the boss of the gang. Certainly, she knew of the boy's activities and did not object, and must have participated to some extent. But whether she actually planned their crimes, as she has been accused, is unknown. The rumor is that Ma told the boys, "do whatever you want. Just don't get caught." Obviously the boys did not listen to their mother.

Doc was arrested in 1918 for stealing a car that belonged to the Government. He broke out of jail and with Ma's help, managed to stay hidden for two years. He was arrested again, in 1920, for killing a night watchman at St. John's Hospital in Tulsa while attempting to steal a drug shipment. In spite of Ma's attempts to rescue him, he was sentenced to life in the Oklahoma penitentiary. He served thirteen years before being paroled in 1932.

Lloyd was arrested for robbing a post office in rural Oklahoma in 1922, and served a twenty-five year sentence at Leavenworth Federal Prison in Kansas. Already in prison, he was the only brother who was not an actual member of the Barker gang.

Herman became a member of the Kimes-Terrill Gang in the early 1920s They robbed banks in Texas, Oklahoma, and Missouri. Herman committed suicide on September 19, 1927, after being trapped by lawmen in Kansas. Ma and George were briefly reunited when they met at the rural cemetery at Welch, Oklahoma, to bury Herman.

Fred, the youngest son, spent some time in an Oklahoma reformatory but Ma was able to get him released. He was arrested for a burglary in Claremore and Ma paid a $10,000 bond for his release. He jumped bail leaving a red-faced Ma with ten thousand fewer dollars. He was arrested in Kansas for robbery and sent to the Kansas State Penitentiary in Lansing. In 1931, he was released and returned to Tulsa bringing with him a fellow convict, named Alvin "Creepy" Karpis. Alvin Karpis, also, later became one of J. Edgar Hoover's most wanted men. Fred and Alvin were arrested by the Tulsa police, on June 10, 1931, for robbing a jewelry store in Henryetta. Fred escaped, but Alvin was sentenced to four years at the Oklahoma State Penitentiary at McAlester.

In the meantime, Ma had taken a lover, a retired billboard painter named Arthur "Old Man" Dunlop, who also moved into the crowded little house. After 21 years of living in Tulsa, Ma decided that Tulsa had become too dangerous for her boys. She moved them back to Missouri where Fred and Alvin promptly murdered a local sheriff.

They moved again, this time to St. Paul, Minnesota. The son of their landlord recognized their pictures from a detective magazine and turned them into the police. Tipped off that the police were going to raid their house they escaped again. Fred and Alvin thought that Ma's boyfriend had tipped off the police, so they shot him and threw his body in a lake. When the body was identified, warrants went out for Fred, Alvin, and Ma.

The gang fled to Kansas City, where more bank robberies and killings occurred. They returned to Tulsa, where Ma became upset with a lawyer who was to defend one of the captured gang members. She made a date to meet the lawyer at the Indian Hills Country Club. The day after that, the police found his body.

Ma and the boys went back to Minnesota, robbing banks in Kansas along the way. In December of 1932, the boys killed two policemen during a bank robbery in Minneapolis.

Governor "Alfalfa" Bill Murray signed a banishment parole (paroled on condition of leaving the state) for Doc. He and some of his buddies from McAlester joined the gang in St. Paul. The gang had grown and Ma was said to lead the gang with an iron hand.

The next few years were a series of bank robberies, holdups, kidnappings, and killings in several states.

By 1934 the FBI had a concerted effort to rid America of the criminal element that had overtaken the country. The Federal Bureau of Investigation listed Ma Barker on its "most wanted" list.

Of all the violent criminals of that time, Ma Barker, more than any other, attracted the wrath of FBI Director, J. Edgar Hoover, who found her to be a cold-blooded creature of evil. He described her as, "the most vicious, dangerous, and resourceful criminal brain of the last decade... The eyes of Arizona Clark Barker always fascinated me. They were quietly direct, penetrating, hot with some strangely smoldering flame, yet withal as hypnotically cold as the muzzle of a gun. That same dark, mysterious brilliance was in the eyes of her four sons."

The FBI declared an all out "War on Crime." In 1934, the newspapers were filled with the obituaries of the tough killers that had made the FBI's most wanted list. Bonnie and Clyde, who had included Oklahoma in their bloody trek across the southwest, were gunned down May 23, 1934. John Dillinger was killed July 22, 1934. Oklahoma folk hero, Charles "Pretty Boy" Floyd, was killed October 22, 1934, and on November 28, 1934, "Baby Face" Nelson met his death in a gunfight with federal officials outside Chicago.

On January 16, 1935, Ma and Fred Barker were killed, with machine guns in hand, at their hideout at Lake Wier, Florida. The machine gun fight began at 6:45 a.m. and lasted for six hours. Fred had eleven bullet holes in his body and Ma was killed by one bullet in the heart. More than 1500 federal bullet holes were in the house.

Doc, who had been arrested before the gun battle was sentenced to imprisonment on a kidnapping charge and sent to Alcatraz. Three years later he was shot while trying to escape.

Lloyd was released from Leavenworth in 1947, after serving a twenty-five year sentence. He was killed by his wife in 1949.

George Barker, the forgotten husband, brought the bodies of his wife Kate and son Fred back to Welch where they were buried beside Herman. When George died, he was placed beside them. A single headstone marks the grave of all four.

ADA LOIS SIPUEL FISHER

Pioneer of Integrated Education

In Oklahoma in 1945 a white student who attended class with a black student could be fined $20.00 a day. The state law said a teacher who taught a racially mixed class could be fined $50.00 and a president of a university or college who permitted mixed enrollment would be subject to a fine not to exceed $500.00 per day. This was the situation when Ada Lois Sipuel Fisher, who is black, made the courageous decision to follow her dream of becoming a lawyer by applying for admission to the University of Oklahoma School of Law.

Ada Lois Sipuel Fisher entered Monnet Hall, commonly known as the "Law Barn," at the University of Oklahoma. She passed the first two rows where the white students were sitting, and began the slow climb upward to the back of the room. The room was arranged theater style with each row becoming narrower and steeper as it went to the back. Her mind kept saying "step up, step up, step up," as she tried not to concentrate on the students watching her climb. Behind the last row of seats was an old fashioned wooden chair with a sign on it that read, "colored."

Ada took her seat and removed a pencil and paper from her briefcase. She had made it! It had been a long climb but she had made it. She smiled to herself as she thought, "Indeed, it has been a long climb, not just the ascent to the back of the room at Monnett Hall, but a much longer climb, full of peaks and valleys, that had lasted three years." Now she may be in the back of the room, but she was at the top. Her dream was coming true! She was in the freshman class of the University of Oklahoma Law School and she was on her way to becoming a lawyer.

Ada could not remember when she first decided she wanted to be a lawyer. It might have been when as a child, she visited an older cousin who was a lawyer in Chicago. He had a daughter Ada's age and on Saturdays the girls would visit his downtown office and play with the typewriters. Those visits had an early influence on Ada. But she felt the dream was futile for a black girl living in Oklahoma. The only college she could attend was Langston University and the school was not fully accredited and did not offer a law school or any Master's programs.

Ada was born February 8, 1924, in Chickasha, Oklahoma, the daughter of Rev. and Mrs. T. V. Sipuel. Her father was a bishop in the Churches of God in Christ in Oklahoma with twenty-five churches under his jurisdiction. Ada and her brother and sister grew up in an educated household, knowing that an education was the key to success. Ada graduated with honors from Lincoln High School, "the colored school," in Chickasha. She was the class valedictorian. She attended Langston University, earning a degree with a double major in history and English. Still, she dreamed of some day obtaining a law degree.

In 1945, while enjoying her senior year of college, Ada did not realize that events were taking place in Oklahoma that made that dream not quite so impossible. That summer, a meeting of the National Association for the Advancement of Colored People was held in McAlester, Oklahoma. A decision was made to initiate action to end segregation in higher education in Oklahoma.

Attending the meeting was the distinguished black lawyer from New York, Thurgood Marshall. Marshall, as legal council for the NAACP, announced that an attempt would be made to enroll students at the University of Oklahoma, who needed courses at the graduate level, or in professional programs, not offered at Langston University.

Ada Lois Sipuel Fisher in 1992 when appointed to University of Oklahoma Board of Regents. Courtesy of the Black Chronicle.

A statewide search was begun to find just the right plaintiff for the law suit. Ada's family doctor in Chickasha, Dr. W. A. J. Bullock, who was also an officer in the state NAACP, suggested Ada's older brother Lemuel. Lemuel had graduated from Langston three years earlier and then had been called up for service in World War II. He felt he needed to get on with his life and did not wish to be considered. Ada let them know she was very interested. After several weeks of consideration Ada was chosen.

George Lynn Cross, then President of the University of Oklahoma, said as soon as he saw Ada he knew the NAACP had made a wise choice. She was attractive, intelligent, poised, charming, and determined. She also had an excellent scholastic record, was the daughter of a minister, and her husband was in the military. She married Warren Fisher her senior year of college, but because her transcripts were in the name of Sipuel, the law suit was filed under the name of Ada Lois Sipuel. Later, the name Fisher was added to the suit.

On January 14, 1946, Ada, accompanied by Roscoe Dunjee, Editor of *The Black Dispatch*, and Dr. W.A.J. Bullock, Regional Director of the NAACP, walked into the admission office at the University of Oklahoma and asked for admission forms. They were referred to President Cross, who began reciting the state law that prohibited the admission of Negroes to the University. He reminded them that it was a misdemeanor, and not only would he be subject to fine, but would also be putting the faculty and the white students at risk of being fined. During the meeting, a copy of Ada's transcript was sent to the Dean of Admissions for evaluation. Upon receiving his report, Dr. Cross wrote a letter saying that she was academically qualified for admission but could not be admitted solely because of her race. The visitors thanked Dr. Cross and as they were leaving, they were invited to lunch by members of the University's YMCA-YWCA Race Relations Committee.

The admission denial was greatly publicized by local and national news media, and it was announced that Thurgood Marshall would be coming to Oklahoma to file a test suit.

Ada was a little apprehensive about meeting the famed Marshall. She had once heard him deliver a speech in Chickasha and had been awed by his eloquence. Upon their introduction, he immediately gave her a big bear hug, and in a few minutes, they were no longer strangers, but friends "Thurgood" and "Ada."

The case, Sipuel v. Oklahoma, was held at the district courthouse, in Norman, on July 9, 1946, and as was expected, Ada lost the case. An appeal was immediately made to the Oklahoma Supreme Court and was heard on March 4, 1947. Thurgood Marshall pled brilliantly that segregation was a violation of the Fourteenth Amendment and there was no equality under segregated systems. In spite of the impressive presentation, the Oklahoma Supreme Court sustained the ruling of the Cleveland County District Court. Their ruling was that Oklahoma met the requirement of separate but equal by offering out-of-state tuition to blacks who wanted to go beyond the baccalaureate degree.

Ada felt like it made so much sense when Thurgood pled that "Unless you send white people out of state on interstate tuition, you can't send black folk out of there, either." She was very disappointed when the judges did not agree. Thurgood put his arm around her and said, "Don't get discouraged, Ada. We are on our way. The next step is to try to get you before the Supreme Court of the United States. That is the place we will tell the story."

The U.S. Supreme Court accepted the petition, and arguments were heard on January 9, 1948. Ada would never forget the feeling she had upon walking into the chamber of the Supreme Court of the United States, in Washington, D. C.. She was awed by the somberness of the thick carpeting, the big velvet curtain and the Marines standing guard all down the hall.

When the bailiff called "Hear ye, hear ye, the Supreme Court of the United States" and the judges stepped through the curtain and sat down, Ada thought, "I'm dreaming. All of this is because of me."

Four days later, in the fastest decision that the Supreme Court had ever issued, Oklahoma was ordered to provide a legal education for the petitioner as soon as it would be provided for the applicants of any other racial group. But the court did not declare Oklahoma's segregation laws unconstitutional.

Evidently, the court felt that since second semester classes would begin January 29, it would be necessary to enroll her or not enroll any white students, as it would be impossible for the state to provide separate facilities in seventeen days. They underestimated the determination of those Oklahomans involved in the case.

While Ada and her attorneys were rejoicing in the decision, the Oklahoma State Regents for Higher Education were establishing a Langston University School of Law in the State Capitol building, a branch of Langston University. In approximately one week, a dean and two additional faculty members were employed by the new law school, to teach Miss Sipuel.

Understandably, Ada refused to attend the school that was regarded as a joke, and nicknamed the Ada Lois School of Law. So after two years, Ada found herself back where the case had started, the district court of Cleveland County. This time, her attorneys brought experts from all across the country to visit the O.U. Law School and the school at the capitol, and to testify as to their equality. Even after all the expert testimony that the new school was not accredited, did not have full time professors, a law library, or other students, the judge handed down his decision that the schools were equal. An appeal was made to the State Supreme Court with plans to go all the way to the U.S. Supreme Court if necessary.

By this time, the ridiculousness of the situation was becoming apparent. Newspapers were asking the question, "what if a black wanted to enroll in medical school, would the University build a hospital just for his training?" About this same time, six other black students applied to O. U. for master's degrees not available at Langston.

Students at O. U. decided to voice their opinion. Approximately one thousand students assembled north of the administration building to protest the denial of admission of blacks to the University. A copy of the Fourteenth Amendment was shredded and set on fire. The ashes were emptied into an envelope addressed to President Harry S. Truman, whereupon the group, singing "The Battle Hymn of the Republic," marched to the Campus Corner post office and mailed the letter.

Veterans at Langston also wrote President Truman, saying they felt that Blacks fought for the United States during World War II and should be granted the opportunity to attend state schools.

At the urging of President Cross, the O. U. Board of Regents, and the State Board of Higher Regents, the Oklahoma legislature passed a bill which permitted the admission of black students to white colleges when the programs they desired were not available. At the last moment, they added a provision that the instruction must be given under strictly segregated conditions.

Thus, two weeks after the semester had started in 1949, Ada was permitted to attend classes at the O.U. School of Law. All the white students were moved to the front of the room and she was made to sit in the back in a chair marked "colored". At noon, she went through a side door to a table with a long chain around it where she ate her lunch. A big burly guard with a pistol made sure she did not overstep her bounds.

But, if the chain was to keep Ada from joining the white students, it did not stop them from joining her. The students told her how glad they were to see her, offered to loan her books and notes, and promised to meet her under the tree outside and tutor her until she caught up with the class. Before long, Ada formed many good friendships that lasted through the years. Even the professor, who had testified against her, invited her to join his family for lunch at their home and they became good friends.

In 1950, in McLaurin v. Oklahoma State Regents, argued by Thurgood Marshall, the United States Supreme Court issued a landmark decision that blacks would be admitted to graduate study in all state-supported colleges and universities in the country and all restrictions removed. Ada immediately moved to the front of the classroom and accepted her classmates' invitation to sit at their table for lunch.

Ada graduated from the University of Oklahoma Law School in 1951, and passed the state bar examination that same year. A few months after that, her first child, a son, was born. After practicing law for a time in Oklahoma City, Ada accepted a position to teach American Government classes at Langston University. She later became the head of the Department of Social Studies at Langston. Seventeen years after receiving her law degree, Ada was awarded a master's degree in history at the University of Oklahoma.

Forty-five years later, the cycle was completed when on April 28, 1992, Ada Lois Sipuel Fisher was appointed to the University of Oklahoma Board of Regents. Now she was on the governing board of the school that once did not want her as a student. Ada Lois said, "I was so tickled that the school that originally didn't want me had come full circle. I went from the back of the classroom to the board of regents."

Perle Mesta with Oklahoma First Lady Willie Murray at O'Mealley's Capitol Cafeteria, Oct. 31, 1952. From the Johnson Murray Collection. Courtesy of the Archives & Manuscript Division of the Oklahoma Historical Socirty.

PERLE MESTA

"The Hostess With the Mostess"

Perle Mesta combined politics and parties with a zest that was appreciated by ten United States Presidents. Her warm outgoing personality and flair for diplomacy led to her appointment as minister to Luxembourg by President Harry Truman in 1949. She was honored at the 1965 World's Fair by being named Oklahoma's Ambassador to the World.

Perle stood on the deck of the *Liberte'*, the huge ocean liner carrying her back to America. She reread the yellow telegram she held in her hand. Angrily, she stomped her foot. "Just who in blazes do those striped pants boys back in Washington think they are," she muttered to herself. She crumpled the cable and started to throw it overboard into the dark swirling sea below. "No, I'll just show it to the President, himself," she thought.

Having just completed her first year as the United States Ambassador to Luxembourg, Perle was returning to Washington for a briefing with President Truman and the Secretary of State.

The telegram that had prompted her fury was from Under Secretary of State James Webb, with the order that upon her arrival in New York she was to return post haste to Washington, and under no circumstances was she to attend the Broadway opening of *Call Me Madam*.

"I guess the State Department thinks it is beneath their dignity for one of their representatives to be the object of satire," she thought. "But I thought it would be rather fun."

Of course, it was widely known that the life of Sally Adams, the heroine of the play, was very similar to Perle's own circumstances. She was an avid Democrat and a close friend of the President of the United States called Harry. She was also a party-loving Washington hostess and the ambassador to a tiny European duchy. The newspapers had all begun calling Perle "The Hostess With the Mostess," after a song in the play written by Irving Berlin.

Actually, Perle had been very excited when she received front row tickets for the opening night performance from the star Ethel Merman. She had even had a new dress made for the occasion. But obeying orders, Perle was in Washington attending a benefit concert with Mrs. Truman, while the press was looking for her on Broadway.

The next day, Perle went to the President himself, and asked if he objected to her and his wife Bess attending a matinee performance.

The President laughed and said indeed, he did not mind and if he were not so busy he would go with them. He did give Perle a piece of advice, "Do not be offended at any of the lines. It is just a play and they have to make up things or it would not be funny."

The Truman's daughter Margaret was studying music in New York, so Perle and Bess picked her up and entered the theater after the lights had gone down so no one would recognize them. Of course, they also had to have extra seats in front and behind them for the Secret Service who always accompanied the first family.

Perle thoroughly enjoyed the play and laughed when Bess nudged her and said, "That's you!" when they sang "she always gets her guests to perform." Perle winced at the jokes about the President and felt sorry for Margaret when they joked about her getting bad notices for her singing, but the first lady and her daughter laughed good-naturedly.

Some parts of the play were just not true - like Perle falling in love with the foreign minister, and the fictitious town of Lichtenburg asking the United States to pay its debts. Luxembourg had never asked the United States for money. But enough of it was similar to Perle's own life that it brought back a lot of memories. Especially when Sally Adams said, "I want Harry to be proud of me."

In the hotel room that night, Perle lay back on her pillows and thought of the play and her own early years that had brought her to this day in 1950, when she was the Ambassador to Luxembourg and known the world over as "The Hostess With the Mostess."

Perle was born Pearl Skirvin in 1890, the daughter of the wealthy oilman, William Balser Skirvin. Her father had been on one of the first trains coming into Oklahoma Territory during the renowned land run of 1889. The train was so full of land hungry settlers that he was literally on top of the train. He bought and sold several lots in Guthrie and Oklahoma City before going to Texas where he became quite wealthy in the famous Spindletop oil field. Pearl was born in Michigan where her mother, in frail health, had gone to escape the Texas heat. In 1900, William Skirvin moved his family back to Oklahoma City. A few years later, her mother died, after telling Pearl that as the oldest child she would have the responsibility of caring for the family. Perle was always close to her father and smiled fondly as she thought of him now.

William Balser Skirvin was always unpredictable, but in 1910 he embarked on a new venture that was to change all their lives. He decided to build a hotel. Not just any hotel, but the finest in the Southwest. Papa engaged the finest architect in Oklahoma City, Solomon Layton, who also built the state capitol and Central High School. Governor Haskell turned the first spadeful of dirt for the groundbreaking in 1910. The hotel was to be six stories tall, but when the framework for the fifth floor was completed, Papa and Sol had celebrated with a few drinks and decided the hotel was too small so they enlarged it to eight stories. A few weeks later, they got together again to celebrate and the same thing happened again. By September of 1911, when the hotel was finished, it was ten stories high, had two wings, and three hundred rooms. It was the most deluxe hotel in the Southwest, featuring all outside rooms, running ice water in each room, and a ballroom that could seat 500.

Perle chuckled as she thought of how she and her younger sister Marguerite and brother William called the hotel "Papa's 300 room hobby." Papa was like a feudal baron. He had his own gas pipeline and water wells, generated his own electricity, his own laundry and his own garbage disposal plant.

Papa was also unpredictable. He had a rule about no animals in the rooms. Once, when Katherine Cornell was appearing in *The Barretts of Wimpole Street* and staying in the hotel, he would not let her keep her two dachshunds in the room, but insisted they must stay in the kennel in the basement. She refused and stayed in another hotel. But when a lion tamer came with his pet lion that was too large for the kennel, Papa let him keep the lion in his room. Perle laughed to herself as she remembered how scared the maid was when she went to change the linen.

The family kept a suite in the hotel, and although Marguerite and Pearl were usually away at boarding school, they loved staying in the hotel during vacations. No one else had a grand ballroom for their parties!

After boarding schools, Perle moved to Chicago to attend the Sherwood School of Music. Then, in 1915, she moved to New York City to pursue her musical studies. In New York, she lived with a wealthy great aunt in a beautiful apartment on Park Avenue.

At a dinner party, she met a handsome young man named George Mesta. Perle's eyes misted as she thought of George - he was blonde, slim, distinguished looking and 40 years old (almost twice her age.) He asked her out to dinner at the Ritz the next evening. Not knowing his financial status, Perle suggested dinner at Schrafft's and a ride through Central Park. She laughed as she thought of how he tried to talk about engines but not knowing anything about the subject, she switched the conversation to music. "Imagine how I felt," she remembered, "when the next morning I found out he owned the Mesta Machine Company that made the biggest steel machinery in the world, and was worth about 15 million dollars."

After a short but romantic courtship, they were married at her aunt's apartment, honeymooned in Havana, then made their home in Pittsburgh where the business was located. Perle shuddered as she thought of how she hated Pittsburgh. She did not get along with the housekeeper and never really fit in with Pittsburgh society. But she did manage to leave her mark there, as she instituted a day care center at the plant, and organized Christmas parties for all the workers' children.

As the United States became involved in World War I, George's plant began manufacturing naval gun barrels and other war machinery. George became a dollar-a-year consultant to President Wilson. The Mestas took an apartment in Washington, D.C., and divided their time between there and Pittsburgh. Pearl loved the excitement of Washington, and became intrigued with the way the leading hostesses combined politics with parties. Although she seldom gave parties in those days, she attended many.

Perle's eyes filled with tears as she remembered how her life crashed around her when in 1925, George suddenly died of a heart attack. Perle was devastated, but she took over the company business and ran it successfully, as she knew George would want. She floundered for many years after that, with more money than she knew how to spend. She shopped lavishly, went to the races in Saratoga, had homes in Newport, Palm Beach, New York, and Oklahoma City. She began entertaining, mostly with the New York Opera crowd. As an attractive wealthy widow, Perle had many suitors, some of them fortune hunters, and some rather serious - as her relationship with Carl Magee, the Oklahoma City reporter who invented the parking meter. But none were George.

Two years after her husband's death, Perle became politically active when she joined the National Woman's Party and became its Congressional Chairman. The nation's capital soon became her main residence.

In 1944, Perle made two major decisions - she changed the spelling of her name from Pearl to Perle, and her political affiliation from Republican to Democrat. Perle became a businesswoman again, raising cattle in Arizona to alleviate the meat shortages due to the war. Her venture was a great success.

Life for Perle took on more meaning in 1942, when she began volunteering for the USO Canteen in Washington. She smiled as she thought of her good friend Evelyn Walsh McLean, known as the leading Washington hostess of the day, who began entertaining only for American Servicemen. She would take her famous Hope Diamond to the USO and pass it around for the fellows to hold.

It was at this time that Perle also became known as a leading Washington hostess, especially in the political arena. She entertained for President Roosevelt but became especially interested in the young Senator from Missouri, Harry S. Truman. She campaigned relentlessly for Truman and gave parties for him, his wife Bess and their teenage daughter Margaret. After Truman's election in 1948, he called Perle and pleaded with her to take over the arrangements for the Inaugural Ball. One of the most exciting events in her life was entering the National Guard Armory on the President's arm, with the bands playing "Hail to the Chief" and spotlights dancing around them as they walked to the Presidential box, closely followed by Mrs. Truman and the ball co-chairman Edgar Morris.

Perle's entertaining fame grew. She soon found that very often political differences or matters of policy could be worked out in a social atmosphere better than in any board room. Often, it was a matter of mixing the right people at the right time, and Perle soon found that she had just the right talent for organizing such events. She even got up her courage to invite the President of the United States to a small supper party. She was surprised when not only did he attend and have a wonderful time, but he also entertained the guests by playing the piano. He soon became a frequent guest.

Perle could still feel her surprise when the President asked her to accept a diplomatic post as Ambassador to the tiny European Duchy of Luxembourg, which was ruled by the Grand Duchess Charlotte.

The newspapers had a heyday - Perle was criticized strongly as having no credentials. Perle laughed aloud as she remembered the furor the appointment had caused. It was funny now, but it was not at all funny at the time. Reporters asked her if she felt she could ease the cold war by giving parties. She answered, "If giving parties would do it, I would certainly give all the parties I could".

Another asked, "How does one address you now? Your Excellency? Madam Minister? Or what?"

"Oh, just call me Perle," Perle answered.

Perle's arrival in Luxembourg was not as dignified as she had hoped. The American Embassy had provided a driver and a car which met her entourage in Paris and proceeded to lead them to Luxembourg. However, he got lost and they arrived several hours late, long after the dignitaries with their flowers and speeches had gone home. Perle muttered to herself, "I still think some American newspaper reporter had a hand in that mess."

It was not long until Perle discovered she had her work cut out for her. No one really wanted her in Luxembourg. The government officials, while honored that they were recognized by the United States with the appointment of an official minister, were disappointed that it was not someone of more recognized status, let alone a woman. The members of the embassy staff strongly resented the fact that they had been sent a minister who had no training in diplomacy.

About the only encouragement Perle had in the first days was that her sister Marguerite had accompanied her. In fact, it was Marguerite who saved Perle from the same embarrassment that befell Sally Adams in *Call Me Madam*. In the play, Sally had fallen on her derriere when curtseying to Queen Duchess Charlotte. Perle was reminded now of how she and Marguerite had practiced and practiced Perle's formal presentation to the Court. Seated atop two pillows on a Louis XVI armchair, with bracelets on her head simulating a crown, Marguerite had motioned Perle to come forward, then to rise and take a seat next to her. After her brief speech, Perle had risen and left the room. Marguerite immediately called her back, shouting, "You must never turn your back on royalty!" The presentation of the credentials went quite well, and Perle and the Grand Duchess got along quite well, discovering they had many friends in common.

Perle knew it would be difficult and she might make some mistakes in protocol, but she made up her mind that the best thing she could do was be warm and neighborly and convey to the people of Luxembourg her interest and the interest of her country. Each morning she would ask herself, "What can I do today that will help my country and will help Luxembourg?"

What many people did not realize was that Luxembourg, although small, was the sixth largest steel producing country in the world, and Perle's experience with the Mesta Steel Works gave her experience in this area. This knowledge also made her an instant hit with the people. Just recently, Eleanor Roosevelt had written an article for the Cowles Magazine Company, in which she said she had at first questioned President Truman's reason for appointing Perle as ambassador, but upon visiting Luxembourg she had seen how Perle's experience in the steel industry made her very useful in that position. She went on to also compliment her on her friendliness with the people, and in seeing every American who entered the country. She ended the article by saying that Madam Minister demonstrated that women were able to serve not as women but as able representatives of the United States.

Perle and Marguerite set to work redecorating their new residence and Perle began entertaining. She entertained not only the Luxembourg officials but also the burgomasters, who were the district leaders and usually farmers, blacksmiths, miners, or other working class people. Her staff told her they would be uncomfortable, but they did not know Perle was famous for making people feel at ease. She opened the gardens and served them beer and smoked pork and beans. It was very informal, with accordion music in the background. Before long, they were having a wonderful time and calling her Perle.

On weekends, Perle and her sister would drive through the countryside, meeting as many of the people as possible and attending community celebrations and the many small country fairs. Perle not only entertained the Supreme Commander of the NATO forces, General Dwight Eisenhower, and his wife Mamie, but also began her famed G.I. parties. She began holding open house every Saturday for any G.I. stationed in Europe. She entertained over 25,000 American servicemen and women, and often, after the party she would write the parents of the young men and women telling them John or Susie was doing well. At the same time, she began her Youth Argosy Project, in which she brought young American students to Luxembourg, and also gave scholarships to talented Luxembourg students to study in the United States.

Now back in her hotel room, sleep finally came to Perle. It was a peaceful sleep as she thought of how successful her short time in Luxembourg had been and realized just how eager she was to return.

Perle's success was shown shortly before she left Luxembourg in 1953, when the Grand Duchess bestowed on her the Grand Cross of Oak, the country's greatest honor, never before bestowed on a woman. The evening before her departure, the Luxembourgers staged an enormous parade in her honor, and 200 orphan children presented a farewell gift to "Madame Minister, Our American Auntie." She left the country to the echo of a 21 gun salute.

Shortly after, she visited the Soviet Union, at their invitation, to inspect their steel mills. The next few years were quite busy, as Perle traveled around the world lecturing, writing articles, and, of course, giving parties. The biggest party of her career as a hostess was her party in London for the American delegation to Queen Elizabeth's coronation. What started out to be a small dinner ended up with 125 guests for dinner and an additional 575 for the supper dance. Guest ranged from the King of Norway to the Hollywood stars Humphrey Bogart and Lauren Bacall.

Although she was famous as a hostess, she was a Christian Scientist who neither drank or smoked, but she loved a lively game of cards. Perle was said to have wined and dined more VIP's than any other private individual in Washington. In later life, it became important to Perle that her life be remembered as more than one long party. She wanted to be remembered not as a lavish party giver but as a woman who enjoyed bringing together people of mutual interests for specific purposes, and also for her efforts on behalf of woman's rights and better international understanding.

The last two years of her life, she lived in Oklahoma City with her brother William Skirvin. In 1940, she died in Oklahoma City at the age of 50.

Oklahoma was very dear to her. Shortly before she died she was asked which of her many titles - official and nonofficial - she cherished the most. She answered promptly, "My Indian name, Toyoam Ti Toyah Mah, given to me years ago by the Kiowas in Oklahoma. It means, 'Woman Ambassador of Good Will Over The World.'"

TE ATA

"Bearer of the Morning"

Her name was Mary Thompson, or later Mrs. Clyde Fisher; but she was known the world over as simply Te Ata. An actress and story teller of international reputation, she devoted her life to dramatic interpretations of the folklore of the American Indians. In 1987, at the Governor's Art Awards, she was proclaimed Oklahoma's First State Treasure, a bearer of intangible cultural assets.

Te Ata remembered as a small child, sitting indoors on cold nights, begging her father to tell a story. She and the other children would sit by the fire, wrapped in blankets, listening in hushed awe as her father began, "There goes Grandfather Turtle." Her father especially liked telling stories of animals or of the creation of life.

A Chickasaw Indian, Te Ata was born December 3, 1895 in Emet, Indian Territory, and grew up near Tishomingo, the capitol of the Chickasaw Nation. Her parents were Thomas Benjamin and Lucy Alberta Thompson. Her father was the last tribal treasurer elected before statehood, and her uncle was Governor of the Chickasaw Nation. Her father owned a general store that had started out as a trading post. He sold everything from washtubs to saddles, bolts of calico, and food. Many times women brought in eggs and garden produce to trade for household supplies. Te Ata's mother was part Osage and part French. When she was married, her husband paid $50 for her to be given citizenship in the Chickasaw tribe. She was versed in healing herbs and plants and taught her daughter many little known facts of nature.

As a small child, Te Ata had a special talent for dancing and telling stories. In a special ceremony an aunt gave her the name Te Ata meaning, Bearer of the Morning. Te Ata attended a small school for Indians at Emet until she was eight years old, when she was sent to the Indian boarding school, Bloomfield Seminary. Later she finished high school at Tishomingo.

She chose to further her education at the Oklahoma College for Women at Chickasha because it was close to home, was a boarding school, and was not just for Indians. She was very quiet and shy at school. One night some of the girls in her dormitory asked her to tell them some Indian stories. Soon the room was full of girls, sitting on the beds and cross-legged on the floor, listening to her tell them, "why the owl and the rabbit do not get along," and other animal stones. The stories were similar to the ones her father had told her.

Frances Dinsmore Davis, professor of dramatic art, quickly recognized Te Ata's rare talents. She encouraged her to change her major from education to drama. All senior speech and drama majors were required to perform a full evening program for the public. Her teacher suggested to Te Ata that she present a program on Indian lore. For the program she wore a borrowed Plains Indian pale yellow doeskin dress and changed to a Chickasaw calico tent dress for the story telling part of the program. Little did she realize that her senior assignment would lead into a lifelong career of presenting Indian legends and lore.

In the audience was Thurlow Lieurance, a noted composer of Indian music. Lieurance offered Te Ata her first professional tour, a summer on the

Chautauqua circuit. She developed a one woman show of Indian lore accompanied with interpretative Indian dances. This theatrical experience on the road, in the summer of 1919, was an excellent introduction to the world of the stage and the variety

Te Ata. Courtesy of the Oklahoma Heritage Association.

of audiences across the United States.

Te Ata earned enough money on tour to continue her studies in the theater school at Carnegie Institute of Technology in Pittsburgh, Pennsylvania. After a year of school and acting in several little theater productions, she moved to New York City, where she, appeared in several Broadway shows. Her most famous role was Andromache in The Trojan Women. During the summers she continued to do Chautauqua circuits.

Although she enjoyed appearing on the Broadway stage, Te Ata did not enjoy auditioning and competing for roles. Realizing her greatest success and her biggest fulfillment came from her one woman shows, she revived her Indian program. She also felt that she could be of service to her people by depicting the creative and spiritual side of the Indians. She felt that too many people only knew of the Indian war dances around the campfire.

Te Ata traveled around the country gathering a harvest of orations, prayers, chants and songs, legends, and stories passed down through the generations of various Indian tribes. Her appearances, dressed in a variety of beautiful Indian costumes, singing, dancing, and playing the drum, brought to the American people a new appreciation of the history, legends, and humor of the first Americans.

Her pine tree-straight posture and graceful hands created a mystique as if weaving a magical spell upon her audience. With the lift of a shoulder, a change in stance, or a variation in voice she became a warrior, an old woman, a young maiden, a medicine man, or a new mother. In a single performance her audience would rock with laughter and wipe tears of sadness from their eyes. Her stories explained the Indian way of looking at birth, death, love, and the meaning of life.

One of the favorite stories of the audience was how the Great Spirit made the perfect man. She told how the Great Spirit was lonely and wanted to create a perfect man to ease his loneliness. On his first try he used sand to mold the body, shaped the arms and legs, and formed the facial features. But he underbaked him and he was pale and sickly looking. He was disappointed and flung the white man across the ocean. On his second try he used the dirt from beneath the black walnut tree, but he overbaked him. Discouraged he flung the black man across the ocean. On his third try he used the red dirt from beneath the sugar maple tree. As he baked him, he watched very carefully, and took him from the oven at exactly the right time. He was a beautiful golden brown. The Great Spirit was very proud that at last he had created the perfect man - the American Indian.

Te Ata came to the attention of Eleanor Roosevelt, the wife of the Governor of New York. She was invited to give presentations at the Governors mansion and the governor named a lake in New York State Lake Te Ata.

In the spring of 1933, Te Ata was invited to appear at the White House for President Franklin Delano Roosevelt's first state dinner. The guest of honor was Ramsay MacDonald, Prime Minister of Great Britain. After the performance she was invited to spend the night and chose to sleep in the Lincoln bedroom. Many times she was asked by the President to perform at the white house for important guests.

1933 was an exciting year for Te Ata, as that fall she married Dr. Clyde Fisher, curator of the Hayden Planetarium at the New York Museum of Natural History. Although he was older than Te Ata, the two shared many mutual interest, including a love of nature and a fascination with Indian folk-lore. Their marriage, until his death fifteen years later, was a happy time of world travel, fascinating and famous friends, and involvement with the cultural activities of the day.

In 1939, Te Ata was chosen by President and Mrs. Roosevelt to present an American Indian folk-lore program at the Roosevelt family home at Hyde Park, New York, in honor of King George VI and Queen Elizabeth. The King and Queen invited her to appear in England which was the first of many tours throughout Europe.

Te Ata appeared professionally in every state in the nation and many foreign countries. She performed on stage, television, college campuses, schools, museums, and clubs. Her favorite place to perform was on an outside stage. She performed at Carnegie Hall in New York and at the Shakespeare Memorial Theater in England.

She received many honors. In 1957 she was inducted into the Oklahoma Hall of Fame. In 1975, a half-hour documentary film entitled "God's Drum," which presented the life and work of Te Ata was produced. Ladies Home Journal chose her as their "Woman of the Month," in February, 1976. She also appeared on the "Today" show in 1976. She was listed in "Who's Who in America" and named a member of the National Congress of American Indians. In 1976, Governor David Boren and the Arts and Humanities Council named her Oklahoma's first state treasure and honored her as a "bearer of intangible cultural assets, an elder with Oklahoma origins who has outstanding artistic or historical worth."

Te Ata continued traveling and telling her stories until the late 1970s when her health began to fail. She moved back to Oklahoma and continued visiting schools and giving presentations in her native state. At the age of 90 and living in an Oklahoma City nursing home, she still entertained the residents with Indian folk tales. She will be 100 years old this December (1995) and is still a cherished Oklahoma Treasure.

"Let us pause in the stress of our modern life to listen to the ancient lore of our modern land."
Te Ata Fisher

Alice Marriott

ALICE MARRIOTT

"The Story Writing Woman"

Noted for promoting a wider understanding of Native American cultures, anthropologist and author Alice Lee Marriott devoted her life to the study of American Indians and their lives, past and present.

Alice Marriott was the first woman to receive a degree in anthropology at the University of Oklahoma. In addition to two summers' residence among the Kiowa Indians, she devoted more than eight years to the research and writing of these people who had never before told their story.

She was born, January 8, 1910, to a middle-class family, in Willmette, Illinois, a Chicago suburb. The daughter of Richard Goulding and Sydney (Cunningham) Marriott, she was the eldest of five children. Helping raise and entertain her brothers and sisters aided her later in her writing for children.

Her interest in American Indians began at the age of six when her grandfather took her to Chicago's Field Columbian Museum. This natural history museum featured anthropological exhibits from the 1893-94 Chicago World's Fair. While her grandfather visited with the curator, Alice wandered into the basement and discovered some enormous totem poles. Later, her grandfather found her sitting at the foot of one staring at it in awe. Alice remembered this experience as her initial connection with anthropology. "If you found something like that, in unusual circumstances, in childhood, you would just go on following it," she said.

Alice was seven, when her family moved to

Oklahoma City. Her father had accepted a position as the treasurer of an insurance company and her mother worked as a certified public accountant.

Her father was originally from England, and her mother was a southern Virginian. No one in Oklahoma quite understood the family accents. Alice had to learn to speak Oklahoman.

Patricia Loughlin, in her book *Hidden Treasurers of the American West: Muriel H. Wright, Angie Debo, and Alice Marriott,* recounts that the depression of the thirties had consequences for all three ladies, guiding career choices, education, and relationships. In order to save money, Alice lived at home while attending Oklahoma City University. She graduated, magna cum laude, in 1930, with a double major in English and French.

For the next two years she worked as a cataloger for the Muskogee public library. In her autobiography, *Greener Fields: Experiences Among the American Indians* (1953), Alice described the cataloging experience; "The head librarian had a passionate interest in history and genealogy which expressed itself in the form of a collection of books on local history, which in that town meant Indian history. It fell upon me to catalog the books, and subsequently, to index their contents. I discovered in myself an interest in the subjects they covered."

Alice's interest in American Indians grew out of this informative project. She became committed to the study of anthropology. She wanted to attend the University of Oklahoma but discovered the new school of anthropology did not have a graduate program. She enrolled in anthropology I, the freshman course. She also conducted laboratory work in pottery restoration and intensive library research on the archeology of eastern Oklahoma, with the intention of proving through material culture, the relations of pre-Columbian and historical tribes in the region. In 1935, she received her second B.A., as the first woman graduate of the University of Oklahoma's anthropology program.

During her second year at OU, in the summer of 1934 of 1934, Alice received a fellowship from the Laboratory of Anthropology in Santa Fe to study the Modocs in southern Oregon. She was one of two women out of twelve field workers. She wrote her mother that it was, as she predicted: the women worked together and interviewed other women. She began noticing prejudice toward women in her professional field, especially in advancement and pay scale.

From 1938-1942, Alice worked as a field representative for the newly established U.S. Department of Interior Indian Arts and Crafts Board. She traveled constantly, collecting arts and crafts information from Indian tribes all over the United States. Oklahoma was especially challenging as it held the largest Indian population in the United States with 57 federally recognized tribes. An additional difficulty was the general public's lack of awareness of Indian arts and crafts in Oklahoma, in comparison to the arts and crafts of the southwest, particularly Pueblo pottery and Navajo weaving.

This was Alice's first work with the Kiowas and the Plains Indians whom she later spent a great deal of time living with and interviewing. She worked as a specialist in Indian Arts and Crafts with the IACB until because of U.S. involvement in World War II, the field operations were suspended and only nominal work continued at the Washington, D.C. office.

Rather than anthropologist, Alice preferred to call herself an ethnologist. She enjoyed interviewing and then writing for popular appeal among the general public. She is best known for *The Ten Grand-*

mothers, published by the University of Oklahoma Press in 1945. The book tells stories of Kiowa life spanning almost a century from the buffalo days of the mid 1940s to World War II. This history of the tribe tells of their transformation from a nomadic plains tribe to a settled agriculture people. The account is rare in the literature of the American Indian, for it was the Indian's own story, given to the author from the oral tradition of the Kiowas, by the elders of the tribe.

The bulk of her interviews were done in 1934-35 followed by nearly eight years of research. For the rest of her life, she returned to the Kiowa's, living with them for a time. She was even adopted by a Kiowa family.

In *Greener Fields*, Alice explained her relationship with the Kiowa people: "The acid test of an ethnographer's relations with a tribe he has studied is whether or not he can go back. It has always been a matter of pride to me that I could return at will to the group of Indians whom I first studied, and could come and go among them, at once an honored guest and a member of the family. This was true even after I had published two books on the tribe, a time, when if ever, I should have been cast with scoffing into outer darkness."

The Ten Grandmothers met with great praise and is still highly regarded. Criticism that the book was not scholarly enough came from some anthropology societies. But the book was intended to appeal to a general readership. Alice was pleased to receive a note of praise from Angie Debo, stating that it was a "once in a blue moon" kind of book. "I have no words to tell you how much I enjoyed it. I read it slowly savoring every word to make it last longer."

Alice took a position at the University of Oklahoma as associate professor of anthropology from 1942 to 1945, while continuing with her writing.

In 1947, *Winter-telling Stories* and in 1948, *Indians on Horseback* were published, both receiving great critical acclaim.

The University of Oklahoma, in 1949, named her field representative for the Division of Manuscripts of the University Library. She traveled the state, locating documents of historical importance.

One of Alice's most famous books, published in 1948 by the University of Oklahoma Press, was *Maria, the Potter of San Ildefonso.* Maria Martinez, who revived the ancient Pueblo craft of pottery-making, was largely responsible for the current interest in Southwestern Pueblo pottery among both white people and Indians. Maria became, in her own lifetime, a legend.

Among Alice's other books, written for both children and adults, are *Sequoyah: Leader of the Cherokee;, Oklahoma: Its Past and its Present; First Comers: Indians of America's Dawn; Indian Annie: Kiowa Captive; Hell on Horses and Women;* and with Carol K. Rachlin, *Plains Indian Mythology; Peyote;* and others.

Author of over twenty books on biography, ethnology, history, and folklore of Oklahoma, Alice has also written many magazine articles for prestigious publications such as the *New Yorker.*

In 1973, she coauthored with Carol Rachlin, *Oklahoma, the 46th Star.* The book was published by Doubleday and received criticism from the Oklahoma Historical Society for many factual errors. Alice defended the book, saying, "This was never intended to be a history volume. It is a collection of Oklahoma folklore, a record of Oklahoma's development based on recorded and remembered incidents, and was written to be interesting."

Alice later served as artist-in-residence at Central State University and consultant to the Oklahoma Indian Council.

Awards she received include the University of Oklahoma Achievement Award, 1952; induction into the Oklahoma Hall of Fame, 1958; Oklahoma City University Achievement Award, 1968; Key Award from Theta Sigma Pi, 1969; the Oklahoma Literary Hall of Fame, 1972; the Oklahoma Journalism Hall of Fame, 1973,; and the Oklahoma Historians Hall of Fame in 1957,2004. In 1949 she was named "Writer of the Year" by New Mexico Penwomen.

In 1983, Alice was an honored speaker at the dedication of the Kiowa Cultural Center in Anadarko, where her fieldwork had begun more than five decades earlier. The Kiowas were dedicating the center to the "old people who were dead but not forgotten."

In her dedication speech, she discussed her work with the Kiowas: "Perhaps they took pity on me and my ignorance. I'm afraid I had no pity on them. I wanted to learn, learn, learn, whatever they were willing to teach me. I grabbed at every fragment of knowledge, and it all went into the scuffed stenographers notebooks in which I recorded everything. It is still there, although most of it has been bound in books by this time, so that other people may know about the Kiowas."

She reminded her audience that the Kiowa Cultural Center would encourage future generations of Kiowas to learn what the old people tried to teach and wanted to have known.

On March 18, 1992, in Oklahoma City, Alice died when her heart failed. She had, however, lived up to the name given to her by the Kiowa's, "The Story Telling Woman."

MURIEL HAZEL WRIGHT

Keeper of Oklahoma History

Muriel Wright was the granddaughter of Choctaw Chief Allen Wright, the man who proposed the name "Oklahoma" for Indian Territory. She wrote or coauthored 12 books on Oklahoma and served as editor of the Oklahoma Historical Society's Chronicles of Oklahoma from 1943 -1973, shaping it into a well regarded publication.

Muriel Wright has been acclaimed as both making and preserving the history of her state. She described her identity as thoroughly American: one-fourth Choctaw and also from distinguished colonial ancestry. She traced her genealogy to descendents aboard the Mayflower in 1620 and the Anne in 1623.

The oldest of two children of Eliphalet Nott and Ida Belle (Richard) Wright, she was born March 31, 1889 in Lehigh, Choctaw Nation (later Coal County). Her father was half Choctaw Indian; his father, Allen Wright, Chief of the Nation, had married a Presbyterian missionary teacher of colonial ancestry. Muriel's mother, Ida, of English and Scottish ancestry, was a graduate of Lindenwood College in St. Charles, Missouri, who also came to the Choctaw Nation as a Presbyterian missionary.

At the time of Muriel's birth, her father, a graduate of Union College and Albany Medical College, was practicing medicine and serving as company physician for the Missouri-Pacific Coal Mines. In 1903-1905, Dr. Wright also served as president of the Indian Territory Medical Association.

Muriel's grandfather, Reverend Allen Wright played a large role in the history of his people as an educator, leader, and Principal Chief from 1866 to 1870). He was considered "the scholar" of his people. While serving as a Choctaw delegate to Washington at the close of the Civil War, he coined the name "Oklahoma" for the area that was named Indian Territory in the Treaty of 1866. The name meant "Land of the Red Man."

Education was a priority in the Wright family; and in 1895, when Muriel was old enough to enroll in school, they moved to Atoka, a major town in the region. There she attended Presbyterian and Baptist Academy elementary schools until 1902. The family then returned to their farm near Lehigh, and Ida Wright tutored her two daughters at home. In 1906, Alice went east to school, entering Wheaton Seminary, later Wheaton College, in Norton, Massachusetts. She excelled in her studies.

Her family moved to Washington, D.C. in 1908, serving as resident delegate of the Choctaw Nation to the United States Government. Muriel joined them and studied privately, taking French, piano, and voice lessons. When the family returned to Lehigh, she enrolled and graduated from the newly founded East Central State Normal School in Ada, Oklahoma.

Upon graduation, she embarked in a teaching career. Her first position was in Wapanucka, and after a year at nearby Tishomingo, Muriel returned to Wapanucka as high school principal. She also taught Latin, English, and history, coached the girl's basketball team and directed the senior play.

Desiring further education, she began work on a master's degree in English and history at Barnard College, Columbia University, in New York City. The outbreak of World War I forced her to return to Oklahoma in 1917. She served as principal of the Hardwood District School in Coal County, introducing an assistance program for children who could not afford school supplies.

Although, she enjoyed teaching school, Muriel Wright devoted most of her career to researching and writing about the Oklahoma Indians and their role in shaping the history of the state, the West, and American culture. What began as a hobby became her lifelong career.

Among Muriel's literary achievements is the four-volume work *Oklahoma: A History of the State and Its People* (1929) written with Joseph B. Thoburn. This was and still is the most comprehensive study of the state's history and biography.

That same year she wrote *The Story of Oklahoma*, a textbook for public school children. Oklahoma's state textbook commission adopted the book for the public schools, and by 1939 it had sold over twenty thousand copies and had gone through several editions.

The state textbook commission also adopted two more of Muriel's books, *Our Oklahoma* (1939) and *The Oklahoma History* (1955). Joseph Thoburn said of her textbooks, "A fact worthy of mention is that this book is the first history of Oklahoma that has been entirely planned and written by a native of the state, one who has been a successful teacher in the public schools and one, who, in her own personality, combines much that is best and most desirable in both the Caucasian and Native American elements of its citizenship."

Muriel received a grant from the Rockefeller Foundation to prepare *A Guide to the Indian Tribes of Oklahoma.* Published in 1951, this reference work was cited for distinction by the American Association for State and Local History.

In August of 1929, she began working in the research department of the Oklahoma Historical Society on temporary assignment for a special project, researching the Choctaws and Chickasaws. This project was started by former governor and OHS board member Robert Williams to collect biographical material on the "pioneers of Oklahoma." For two years, she worked toward the development of historical data on Indians of Oklahoma. She assisted in an OHS sponsored Chickasaw dictionary. Original manuscripts and letters of early missionaries,

Muriel Hazel Wright

traders, and natives were procured by her for the historical society.

After working several temporary assignments at OHS she was given the permanent position as associate editor of the *Chronicles of Oklahoma* in 1943, then as editor until 1973. Editing this magazine brought her national recognition as she shaped it into a well regarded publication. In this position she was able to emphasize the role of the Indian in the history of the state.

Her own writing which appeared in the Chronicles and many other publications was praised for it's depth of research, personal interviews, insight, and creativity. Over 135 articles have her by-line, many of which received national recognition.

In an article in the Tulsa Tribune, she was asked who she thought was the most historical character in the state. Her answer was, "I think perhaps Bill Murray, but then again, I think it was my grandfather."

Muriel traveled across the state lecturing to adults and speaking to thousands of school children on the benefits of learning history.

Fulfilling a lifetime interest, she was recognized with George Shirk, for a statewide historical marker program. By 1958, the complete marker list contained 557 historic sites. She and Shirk compiled and edited *Mark of Heritage: Oklahoma Historical Markers.* This publication focused on 131 historic sites, provided the location and inscription of each marker and included accompanying photographs taken by Muriel or George Shirk.

She collaborated with historian LeRoy Fischer in another historic sites effort in 1966 with "Civil War Sites in Oklahoma," first published in the Chronicles and later as a pamphlet.

After retiring in 1973, from OHS she maintained

an office there, continuing to write and plan future projects. She was honored for her work by the Society board at a dinner. George Shirk, president of the board, presented her with a plaque and said, "The thought of the gap that would have been left in Oklahoma history had it not been for her work makes me shudder."

Among her many honors, Muriel was inducted into the Oklahoma Hall of Fame in 1940, and received a distinguished Service Citation form the University of Oklahoma in 1949 for her historical writing, civic work, and service to her tribe. In 1951, she was named the Oklahoma City Woman of the Year, and in 1971, was named outstanding Indian Woman of the twentieth century by the North American Indian Women's Association. In 1993, she became the first woman inducted into the Oklahoma Historians Hall of Fame.

She suffered a stroke in 1975 and was hospitalized at St. Anthony's Hospital in Oklahoma City. Feeling her death was near, Dr. Wright called to her bedside, former President of the State Historical Society, now Mayor of Oklahoma City, George Shirk. Muriel told him she was writing two books, but felt she would be unable to complete them. One was *Geronimo*, a geography, and he other *Western Boundary Surveys*, a factual book about surveying of the frontier. Shirk assured her that he would finish them.

At the time of her death, a week later, she was president of the American Indian Hall of Fame in Anadarko and was responsible for the thirty statues of famous Indians now at the Hall. She was also Director Emeritus of the Oklahoma Historical Society, a position no other women has ever held.

Muriel Wright left her legacy in her writings and in her preservation of the history of the state she loved.

MABEL BOURNE BASSETT

Mother to the State's Unfortunate

"To be a real mother to the unfortunate of this state – that is the ambition of Mrs. Mabel Bassett of Sapulpa, democratic nominee for the office of state Commissioner of Charities and Corrections, if she is elected on November 7" according to an article in the Daily Oklahoman in 1923. Indeed, Mrs. Bassett was elected and held the position for six terms, serving the people of Oklahoma until 1947.

Mabel Bourne Bassett was destined to be a crusader. She was born in Chicago, Illinois, August 16, 1876, the only child of Stephen Bourne, a merchant and Civil War Veteran and Martha Tomlin Bourne, an activist for women's rights. Martha, with her sisters, Mary and Margaret, were the first women in the United States to edit a newspaper. The publication, *The Balance,* established in 1870 in Chicago burned in the great fire. It was reestablished and used to champion women's interest and further woman's suffrage. Martha Bourne wrote under the *nom de plume* of "Capitola", and she wrote tirelessly in an effort to free woman of that day from "servitude to citizenship."

She trained her daughter, Mabel to be a public speaker. At ten years of age, Mabel spent the summer in Chautauqua with the humorist Bill Nye. Mabel's education was a practical one in social service. Her formal education was completed at the Missouri School of Social Economy in St. Louis, Missouri.

Mabel married Joseph Bassett, a railroad conductor, in Billings, Montana. In 1902, the couple, with their three children, moved to Sapulpa, Oklahoma. In 1910, they established the new state's first humane organization for children, the Creek County Humane Society. She worked with the juvenile court and with city and county officials in charity work and in the handling of cases where women and children were concerned. A number of glass plants were located in Creek County which made her give special attention to the child labor law. Mabel ran the organization for twelve years and became aware of needed legislation and social reforms

All the while, she dreamed of opening a children's home where many who came under the jurisdiction of the county might find shelter and care, for a little while. A wealthy oil man made that dream possible by turning over to the humane society a cottage equipped to house eight children. In less than a year the society acquired a twelve-room house, and the Creek County Children's Home was founded. This home was one of the model institutions in the state.

The children were not institutionalized but attended public school, church and Sunday School with other children. They were involved in Scouts and other community activities.

After two unsuccessful attempts, Mabel was elected Commissioner of Charities and Corrections in 1922. She was well liked, and in the 1926 elections carried 73 of the 77 counties in the primary, and led the state ticket in the general election. Charged with protecting orphans and inmates of mental and correctional institutions, this office held only investigative power.

Commissioner Bassett worked hard to promote fair living conditions and opportunities for the state's inmates. She was responsible for a bill requesting a new building for women prisoners at the state penitentiary at McAlester. She worked for the passage of a bill creating the Industrial School for Negro Boys at Boley, claiming the boys didn't belong in prison. Under her leadership, in 1944, the state Pardon and Parole Board was created in an effort to establish a more equitable system for inmates to be reviewed for a pardon, leave or parole.

Mabel Bourne Bassett

Mabel was instrumental in the statute, making wife and child desertion a felony, enacted by the Eighth Legislature. She said this would put a check on irresponsible husbands, who without making provision for their families, took off for parts unknown. No partiality for females was intended. She felt a mother who left her children should also be held responsible and punished.

Untiring, she raised the standards of every institution in the state, whether orphanage, mental institution or penal and correctional institution, often with woefully inadequate appropriations. Mabel fought against a wall of prejudice to educate the public in more enlightened treatment of its wards.

Mabel ran on the Democratic ticket for Congress in 1932, but was defeated by a Moore schoolteacher named Will Rogers.

In 1942, in what was viewed as the upset of the statewide election season, she lost the office of Commissioner of Charities and Corrections to Buck Cook. She ran again for the position in 1950, and again lost to Cook.

Mabel then retired to her farm west of Guthrie where she established a model dairy farm with registered Guernseys.

Civic minded, she held offices in, or was a member of the following organizations: Vice-President of the American Prison Association, member of the Police Officer's Association, Big Sisters Organization, Women's Auxiliary of the International Railroad Conductors Union, Farmer's Union, and many Labor organizations. She was affiliated with Eastern Star, the Ruth Bryan Owen Club, Jeffersonian Club, Women's Democratic Council, and Daughters of Democracy.

For her Red Cross work during World War I, Mabel was awarded the highest honor in the state by the National Red Cross, a service medal for 3200 hours of dedicated Red Cross work.

Mabel was inducted into Oklahoma's "Hall of Fame" by the Oklahoma Memorial Association on Statehood Day, November 16, 1937, for her outstanding services for the betterment of mankind.

On August 3, 1953, by direction of Acting Governor James E. Berry, Mabel Bourne Bassett returned to the Capitol, where she had served so faithfully, there to lie in state in the Blue Room. The public mourned her passing. Christian Science services were held for her the following day with burial in Memorial Park Cemetery in Oklahoma City.

In 1977, the office of Commissioner of Charities and Corrections became a part of the new Corrections Department.

A women's correctional center in McCloud bears the name Mabel Bassett, today.

Bibliography

AUGUSTA METCALFE

Harrel, Melvin. "My Life In The Indian Territory of Oklahoma: The Story of Augusta Corson Metcalf." *The Chronicles of Oklahoma*, Vol. XXXIII No. 1 (Spring 1955).

Randall, Katharine. "Pioneer Staked Her Claim On The Beauty in Oklahoma." *The Oklahoma Farmer Stockman*. September 1961.

"The Story Pictures of Augusta Metcalfe." *Oklahoma Today*. Vol. X, No. 3, Summer 1960.

Stewart, Roy. "Sagebrush Artist." *Oklahoma Today*. Winter, 1957.

Stewart, Roy. "Sagebrush Painter." Features. *Daily Oklahoman*. Sunday, April 10, 1949

"Cowhand and the Lady." *Life Magazine*. Chicago. July 17, 1950.

"Pioneer Painter." Original script for WKY T.V. Interview with Gene Allen.

Augusta Metcalfe's Scrapbooks

Personal interview with Howard Metcalfe, son of Augusta.

ALICE BROWN DAVIS

Cornelius, Frankie. "America's First Woman Chief." *Oklahoma Yesterday, Today, and Tomorrow*. Guthrie, Ok., Co-operative Publishing Co. Dec. 1930

Foreman, Carolyn. *Indian Women Chiefs*. Washington, D. C., Zenger Publishing Co. 1954. pages 62-67.

Gasbarino, Merwyn S. *The Seminole Indians of North America*. New York. Chelsea House Publications. 1989.

McReynolds, Edwin C., *The Seminoles*. Norman. University of Oklahoma Press. 1957.

"Death Claims Mrs. Alice B. Davis." *The Daily Oklahoman.* June 21, 1935.

"Seminole Lady Chief has Colorful Career in Affairs of Tribe." *The Daily Oklahoman*, June 22, 1935.

"Hall of Fame to get Bronze Bust of Alice Davis." *The Anadarko Daily News*. Friday, Oct. 16, 1964.

Alice Brown Davis Collection and Pearl Dovell Collection at Archives, Oklahoma Historical Society.

DR. THERESA HUNT TYLER

Murdoch, Thomas J. D.D.S.. "Theresa Hunt Tyler: Watonga's First Resident Dentist." *Oklahoma Dental Association Journal.* Winter 1988.

Ruth, Kent. "Women Doctors Recalled, Window on the Past." *The Daily Oklahoman.*

"First Dentist Was a Woman." *Watonga Republican.* September 11, 1952.

Personal interview and scrapbooks of Hugh Tyler, Dr. Tyler's son.

MIGNON LAIRD

Allen, Robert B., "Mignon Laird From Pullman to Airport." *The Daily Oklahoman.* March 26, 1967.

"Dr. Laird Lived a Long and Colorful Life." *The Altus Times.* May 22. 1985.

Ray, Dee Ann. "Mignon Laird's Legacy Returns to Western Oklahoma." *Cheyenne Star.* November 8, 1984.

_____. "Cheyenne to Observe Special Services for Laird Family." *Sayre Journal.* May 19, 1985.

_____. "Laird Services Monday." *Sayre Journal.* May 22, 1985.

Shields, Donna. "A Tribute to Mignon Laird." *The Sentinel Leader.* June 6, 1985.

Diaries of Mignon baird and Elbertme Laird Newspaper clippings, and press notices. Mignon Laird collection. Archives and Manuscript Division of Oklahoma Historical Society.

Personal interview with Jiggs Kromer and Howard Metcalfe, personal friends of Mignon Laird.

Mignon baird collection, Black Kettle Museum, Cheyenne, Oklahoma.

Curtain Call for Mignon Laird. video cassette. OHS.

ANGIE DEBO

Baird, W. David and Goble, Danny. "Angie Debo." *The Story of Oklahoma.* Norman. University of Oklahoma Press. 1994.

Brown, Opal. "Dr. Angie Debo, Historian of Controversy- Historian of Note." *Oklahoma's Indomitable Women.* Oklahoma City. Oklahoma Heritage Association.

Browning, Boo. "Our Past is People." *Oklahoma Monthly.* November 1977.

Cozby, J. Louis. "Turning 92 Doesn't Slow Down Dr. Debo." *Guthrie Daily Leader.* January 28, 1982.

Cronley, Connie. "Miss Floy's Disciplinarian." *Oklahoma Monthly.* April 1977.

Debo, Angie." A Biographical Sketch by Herself." Vertical file.OHS

Debo, Angie. *Oklahoma Footloose and Fancy Free.* Connecticut, Greenwood Press.

Debo, Angie. *And Still the Waters Run.* Princeton. Princeton University Press. 1972.

Debo, Angie. *Prairie City, the Story of an American Community.* New York. A.A. Knopf, 1944.

Debo, Angie. *The Road to Disappearance.* Norman. University of Oklahoma Press 1934.

DeFrange, Ann. "Along the Way, History Just Happened to Miss Angie." *The Daily Oklahoman.* April 7, 1985.

MacKenzie, David. "Documentary Records Career of Angie Debo." *Tulsa World.* April 1, 1994.

McNutt, Michael. "State Slights Own, Debo Says." *The Daily Oklahoman.* November 1O 1987.

State Historian Angie Debo to be Buried in Marshall." *The Daily Oklahoman.* February 23, 1988.

"Debo Recalled as Keen Observer Striving for Historical Accuracy." *The Daily Oklahoman.* Feb. 25, 1988.

Shropshire, Lola. "Historian Angie Debo .... Eloquent Evanglist for the Indians." *Twin Territories.* Vol 2. No. 6. 1990.

Selected other newspaper articles.

Angie Debo collection. Archives and Manuscript Division, OHS

Indians, Outlaws, and Angie Debo. PBS Documentary. OHS

AUCE ROBERTSON

Foreman, Carolyn." Mrs Ann Eliza Worchester Robertson and Her Daughter Honorable Alice M. Robertson. article in Alice Robertson file at Oklahoma Historical Society Archives.

Foreman, Carolyn. "Oklahoma Pioneer." *The Delta Kappa Gamma Bulletin.* March 1946 and June 1946.

Litton, Gaston, PH.D. *History of Oklahoma At the Time of Statehood.* New York.Lewis Historical Publishing Co. 1957.

Mazuindar, Maitreye, "Alice's Restaurant:Ezpanding a Woman's Frontier. *The Chronicles of Oklahoma.* Vol.LXX No.3. Fall 1992.

Montgomery, T., Mosier,Lotta, and Bethel, Imogene. "Miss Alice Robertson - Oklahoma's First Congresswoman." *The Growth of Oklahoma.* OKC. The Economy Publisher, 1933.

"A Woman Who Got Into Congress Through the Want-Ad Columns." *The Literary Digest.* December 4, 1920.

Robertson, Alice. "Robertson, Alice Mary of Oklahoma." unpublished autobiography in vertical file, Oklahoma Historical Society archives.

Rogers, Will. "Will Rogers Sez." *Muskogee Times Democrat.* July 3, 1931.

"Miss Alice Was Always There." *Twin Territories.* Vo12. Muskogee. Nov. 7,1902.

"Oklahoma Mourns Miss Alice's Death. *Muskogee Daily Phoenix.* Muskogee, Thurs. July 2, 1931.

"City Pays Last Honor to Miss Alice Robertson. *Muskogee Times Democrat,* July 3, 1931.

Stanley, Ruth Moore. "Alice M. Robertson; Oklahoma's First Congressman." *The Chronicles of Oklahoma.* Vol. XLV.No.3,1967.

Wright, Muriel and Thoburn, Joseph. *The Story of Oklahoma.* Webb Publishing Co. OKC,1929.

THE HARVEY GIRLS

Armitage, Susan and Jameson, Elizabeth (Editors). Spence, Mary Lee. "Waitresses in the Trans-Mississippi West: Pretty Waiter Girls,Harvey Girls and Union Maids." *The Women's West.* Norman. University of Oklahoma Press. 1984.

Foster, George H. and Weiglin, Peter C. *The Harvey House Cookbook.* Atlanta. Longstreet Press. 1992.

Poling-Kempes, Lesley. *The Harvey Girls, Women Who Opened the West.* New York. Paragon House.

Tour and Interview with curator and waitress at Harvey House Cafe, Hugo Heritage Railroad and Depot Museum.

RUBY DARBY

Fenner, Theodoaia,"The Legend of Ruby Darby." *Oklahoma's Historical Edition Vol JH,Diamond Jubilee,1907-1982.* Oklahoma Statehouse Reporter.1982.

Johnson, Caroline. "Show Girl's Daughter 'a Ruby Darby Jr.' *The Tulsa Tribune Tempo.* Friday, May 6,1977.

Michaela, Marilyn. "Ruby Darby." *Oklahoma Today.* Vol.24 number 4. Autumn 74.

Stefanie, Vern."New Musical -Girl With the Blues' Provides New Experience for Theater Students at Tulsa? *The Cue: Official*

*Magazine of Theta Alpa Phi National Theater Honors Frater-
nity.* Vol. 3. page 4.
Wallace, Michael. *Oilman.* New York. Doubleday, New York.
1988.
Selected newspaper articles from appearances in Oklahoma
Ruby Darby's personal scrapbook containing pictures and ar-
ticles, given to Theater Professor Frederick Graves by Ruby
Derby, Jr.
Personal interview with Frederick Graves

MARLAND, LYDE ROBERTS

Allen, Robert B. "Lydie Marland: Veil of Mystery Tight." *The Daily
Oklahoman,* March 1, 1976.
Abercrombie, Louise. "Former State First Lady Dead at 87." *The
Ponca City News,* July 27, 1987.
Abercrombie, Louise. "Lydie Marland Remembered at Memo-
rial Service." *The Ponca City News,* Friday, August 7, 1987.
Abercrombie, Louise. "Long-Lost Statue of Lydie Marland Re-
covered." *The Ponca City News,* Tuesday, May 15, 1990.
Baird, W. David and Gobel, Danny. *The Story of Oklahoma.*
Norman: University of Oklahoma Press, 1994.
"Lydie's Legend." *Oklahoma Today,* May 1995.
Cronley, Connie. "Much Lost Love." *Oklahoma Monthly,* Febru-
ary 1977.
DeFrange, Ann. "Mystery Buried With Former First Lady." *The
Daily Oklahoman*, Friday, August 7, 1987.
Gregory, Bob. "The Legendary Men of Oil." *Oklahoma Monthly,*
February 1976.
Kobler, John. "Where is Lyde Marland?" *The Saturday Evening
Post,* November 22, 1958, pp. 19-20, 44, 47, 51, 52.
Lyde Marland Mystery." *Oklahoma Monthly,* January 1981.
Marland, Lydie Roberts. File at Archives and Manuscript Divi-
sion, Oklahoma State Historical Society.
Matthews, Louise. *The First Ladies of Oklahoma 1907-1991 Dress
Collection.* Oklahoma City: Alpha Press, Inc., 1989.
Matthews, John Joseph. *Life and Death of an Oilman.* Norman:
The University Press, 1951.
Ruth, Kent and Argo, James. "Marland Mansion (The Villa),"
and 'Pioneer Woman Statue." *Window on The Past.* Oklahoma
City: Oklahoma Historical Society, 1984.
Standard, Jim. "Lyde Marland Still Running." *The Oklahoma City
Times,* November 17, 1961.
Wallace, Michael. *Oilman.* New York: Doubleday, 1988.

Wise, Lu Celia. "Lydie Roberts Marland," *Oklahoma's First Ladies*. Perkins, Oklahoma: Evans Publications, 1983.
Tour of Marland Estate

NORMA SMALLWOOD

Cronley, Connie."Much Lest Love." *Oklahoma Monthly*. Feb.1977.
Milsten, David Randolph. *Thomas Gilcrease*. Tulsa. Coman and Associates. 1991.
"Unbobbed School Girl Crowned Miss America." *Miami Daily News*. September 12, 1926.
Norma Smallwood Crowned Miss America. *Tulsa World*. September 12, 1926
Miss America May Go on Stage for Year Only. *The Daily Oklahoman*. September 12, 1916.
Tulsa Gives Keys to Miss America. *New York Times*. Oct.1, 1926.
"Norma's Beauty Not Free." *Tulsa World*. September 9, 1927.
"She is not Money Mad." *Tulsa Daily World*. September 10,1927.
"Our Queens." *The Sunday Oklahoman*. November 12, 1967.
"Most Former Miss Oklahoma's Find Fame a Fleeting Thing." *Tulsa Daily World*. June 7, 1968.
"Miss America Dies." *The Oklahoma City Times*. May 9, 1966.
Norma Smallwood and Thomas Gilcrease scrapbooks - Tulsa Historical Society.

JANE PHILLIPS

Devlin, Jeanne M. "Woolaroc; The Ranch that Frank Built Inspires A New Book." *Oklahoma Today*. November-December 1991.
Frank Phillips Family genealogy and Phillips home chronology
Frank Phillips Collection, Archives and Manuscripts Division OHS
Gregory, Bob. "The Legendary Men of Oil." *Oklahoma Monthly*. February 1976.
Jones, Billy. *L. E. Phillips, Banker, Oilman, Civic Leader*.
"Name Uncle Frank has new meaning after Phillips Party." *Tulsa World*. February 18, 1946.
Selected newspaper articles
Interview with Sue Lacy, curator of Frank Phillips home.
Wallace, Michael. *Oilman*. New York. Doubleday. 1988.
Williams, Joe. *Woolaroc*. Bartlesville. The Frank Phillips Foundation. 1991.

FIVE INDIAN BALLERINAS

Aiken, Charolette "Six Inducted into Oklahoma Hall of Fame." *The Daily Oklahoman*. November 17, 1991,

"All Five State Ballerinas to Attend Mural Dedication." *The Daily Oklahoman*. November 15, 1991.

Chouteau, Yvonne Biography. Oklahoma Heritage Association Files.

Davis, Sandi. "Painting Honors Indian Ballerinas." *The Daily Oklahoman*. November 18, 1991.

Dodd, Craig. Ballet. Secaucus, New Jersey. Chartwell Books. 1979.

deLeeuw, Adele. *Maria Tallchief, American Ballerina*. Champaign, Illinois. 1971.

Flight of Spirit Dedication and program. State Arts Council of Oklahoma.

Larkin, Moscelyne. File at Oklahoma Heritage Association.

Reynolds, Nancy and Reimer, Susan. *Dance Classics, A Viewers Guide to the Best Loved Ballets and Modern Dance*. Chicago. A Capella Books. 1991.

The Simon and Schuster Book of the Ballet. New York. Simon and Schuster. 1979.

Siens, Kenneth L. "From Oklahoma To The International Stage." *The Oklahoma Gazette*. March 15, 1989.

Tallchief, Marjorie. File at Oklahoma Heritage Association.

Tallchief, Maria. File at Oklahoma Heritage Association.

Taper, Bernard. *Balenchine, A Biography*. New York. Time Books. 1984.

Interviews with Yvonne Chouteau and Moscelyne Larkin.

Selected newspaper clippings

Audio tape recordings of interviews with Yvonne Chouteau and Maria Tallchief, Living Legend Library. Oklahoma Christian College.

Video cassette interview with Mike Larson and Yvonne Chouteau by Roger Harris, Oklahoma Historical Society.

COLONEL ROSEMARY HOGAN

"Colonel Rosemary Hogan." *History of Tillman County,* Volume II. Tillman County Historical Society. Frederick, Oklahoma. 1978.

"Rosemary Hogan of Chattanooga Injured in Japanese Bombing." *Grandfield Enterprise*. April 16, 1942.

Maxwell,Carolyn. "Now and Then." *Frederick Press*. January 20, 1977.

Watson, Louise. "I Remember When." *Big Pasture News.* Grandlield. March 16, 1995.

FERN McFARLAND

"40 Years Ago in Seminole." *Seminole Producer.* August 18, 1976.
"Another Downtown Improvement." Seminole Producer. September 16, 1965.
Bryan, Jane. "The Birth of A Boomtown, Seminole, Oklahoma." Thesis found in the vertical file. OHS.
Caldwell, Watson L. "Seminole, Bowlegs, and Little River." *Old West,* Volume II, No. 5. Fall 1975.
"Granny Fern Day Celebrated." *Seminole Producer.* January 2, 1966.
Fulkerson, Jo Ann. "Ray and Fern McFarland's 50th Anniversary Party. *The Daily Oklahoman.* October 5, 1984.
"Funeral Rites Set for Granny Fern." *Seminole Producer.* October 28, 1988.
Phillips, Ted. "Publisher's Comments -One Point of View." *Seminole Producer.* Oct. 30, 1988.
Welsh, Louise; Townes, Willa Mae; and Morris, Jack. *The Greater Seminole Oil Field.* Oklahoma City. Oklahoma Heritage Association. 1981.
Scrapbooks and Interview with Marquita Johnson (Ferns daughter)
Interview with Gb Fortune (Fern's Sister)

KATE "MA" BARKER

Argo, Burnis and Ruth, Kent. *Oklahoma Historical Tour Guide.* Carpenteraville, Illinois. Crossroads Communications. 1992.
Demaris, Ovid. *The Director. An Oral Biography of J. Edgar Hoover.* New York. Harper's Magazine Press. 1975.
Pooter, M. Aurelius. "That Fabulous Barker Bunch." *The Oklahoma Gazette.* Oklahoma City. January 12, 1995.
Prassel, Frank. *The Great American Outlaw. A Legacy of Fact and Fiction.* Norman. University of Oklahoma Press. 1993.
Quimby, Myron J. *The Devil's Emissaries.* A. S. Barnes and Company. 1969.
Ruth, Kent. *Oklahoma Travel Handbook.* Norman. University of Oklahoma Press. 1977.
Ruth, Kent and Argo, Jim. *Here We Rest: Historic Cemeteries of Oklahoma.* Oklahoma City. Oklahoma Historical Society. 1986.

Summers, Anthony. *Official and Confidential: The Secret Life of J. Edgar Hoover.* New York G. P. Putnam's Sons.

Wallace, Michael. *Pretty Boy: The Life and Times of Charles Arthur Floyd.* New York. St Martin's Press. 1992.

"Fred Barker and Mother Killed in Federal Raid? *The Daily Oklahoman.* January 16, 1933.

ADA LOIS SIPUEL FISHER

Aldrich, Gene. *Black Heritage of Oklahoma.* Edmond. Thompson Book and Supply Company. 1973.

Cross, George Lynn. "Guess Who's Coming to School? *Oklahoma Monthly.* September 1976.

Franklin, Jimmie Lewis. *The Blacks in Oklahoma.* Norman: University of Oklahoma Press. 1980.

Grimes, Angie. "Just the Right PlaintiflAda Lois Sipuel Fisher." Interview of Ada Lois Sipuel Fisher for graduate thesis for Oklahoma State University. November 12, 1993.

Henry, Robert. "Retiring One of the State's Legends." *Oklahoma Gazette.* April 15, 1993.

Rowan, Carl T. *Dream Makers, Dream Breakers: The World of Thurgood Marshall.* Boston. Little, Brown & Company 1993.

Swain, Ruth. *Ada Lois: The Sipuel Story.* New York: Vantage Press. 1978

Teal, Kay M. *Black History in Oklahoma: A Resource Book.* Oklahoma City Public Schools. 1971.

Selected Newspaper articles from 1946 to 1950 from *The Daily Oklahoman and The Normman Transcript.*

English, Paul. "New OU Regent Appointment Ends 45-Year Cycle." *The Daily Oklahoman.* April 28, 1992.

Davis, Sandi. "Taking A Stand?" *The Daily Oklahoman.* February 26, 1995.

Telephone Interview with Ada Lois Fisher

PERLE MESTA

Mesta, Pule and Cahn, *Robert Perle: My Story.* New York. McGraw-Hill. 1960.

Meats, Pule *The Encyclopedia Americana.* Vol 18 page 694.

"Perle's Friends." File from the Oklahoma State Department of Libraries on request for a U. S. postage stamp for Perle. Includes biographies and stories of Perle from many noted celebrities including Presidents Jimmy Carter, Gerald Ford, Richard Nixon; Eleanor Roosevelt.

Mesta, Pule file from Oklahoma Historical Society.

Hatch, Katherine. "Perle Whirls Back Home for a 4-Day Visit." *The Sunday Oklahoman.* February 1, 1970.

Heon, Elviretta. "Couldn't Buy Stock in 'Madam' Says Perle." *The Oklahoma Journal.* October 20, 1964.

Hogan, Gypsy. "Holiday Tour Spotlights Mesta Homes." *The Daily Oklahoman.* December 4, 1993.

Mundy, Ann. "Parties, Politicking Perle Mesta's Forte." *The Sunday Oklahoman.* December 1, 1983.

Walker, Elviretta. "Famous Oklahoman Recalls Years as Hostess." *The Oklahoma Journal.* January 26, 1975.

'Perle Meata Still Washington Hostess." *The Sunday Oklahoman.* June 22, 1969.

'Perle Mesta Dead at 85." *The Oklahoma Journal.* March 17, 1975.

"Renowned Hostess Perle Mesta Dies." *The Daily Oklahoman.* March 17, 1975.

TE ATA FISHER

Callahan, Kathy. "She Lives by Beat of a Different Drum." *Tulsa Tribune.* February 12, 1976.

Christensen Harold. "Dr. and Mrs Clyde Fisher." *The Monthly Evening Sky Map.* Brooklyn. 1940.

Devlm Jean. "Te Ata. Bearer Of The Morning." *Oklahoma Today.* January-February 1989.

Sopor, John. "Indian Story Teller Spins Tales of Pride." *The New Mexican.* Santa Fe. June 13, 1971.

Selected other newspaper articles.

File at Oklahoma Heritage Association

Te Ata Collection, Archives and Manuscripts, Oklahoma Historical Societ

"God's Drum," a documentary film of Ta Ata's life and interview on VHS tape, Oklahoma Historical Society.

ALICE MARRIOTT

Loughlin, Patricia , *Hidden Treasures of the American West: Muriel H. Wright, Angie Debo, and Alice Marriott,* University of New Mexico Press, Albquerque, 2005.

Marriott, Alice, *Greener Fields: Experiences Among the American Indians,* Thomas Y. Crowell Co., New York, Ny, 1953.

Marriott, Alice, *The Ten Grandmothers*, University of Oklahoma Press, Norman, OK., 1945.

Marriott, Alice, *Maria, the Potter of San Ildefonso*, University of Oklahoma Press, Norman, OK. 1948.

Marriott, Alice, *Winter-Telling Stories*,Thomas Y. Crowell, New York, NY, 1947.

Marriott, Alice, *Indians On Horseback*, Thomas Y. Crowell, New York, NY, 1948.

Marriott, Alice, *Hell on Horses and Women,* University of Oklahoma Press, Norman,OK, 1953

Marriott, Alice with Caarol Rachlin, Oklahoma: The 46th Star, Doubleday, New York, NY, 1972.

Alice Lee Marriott, Western History Collection, University of Oklahoma, Norman, Ok.

Alice Marriott, Vertical File, Oklahoma Department of Libraries, Oklahoma City, OK

Selected articles from the Daily Oklahoman from the Vertical File, ODL, OKC

Alice Marriott, *Contemporary authors*, p. 373.

Alice Marriott, *Favorite Authors of Books for Boys and Girls*, Thomas Crowell Co.1972

Alice Lee Marriott, Gale Literary Database,

Nomination form for Oklahoma Women's Hall of Fame, Governor's Advisory Committee on the Status of Women,1984.

MURIEL H. WRIGHT

Baird, David and Gobel, Danny, *The Story of Oklahoma*, University of Oklahoma Press, Norman, OK. 1994.

Debo, Angie, *The Rise and Fall of the Choctaw Republic*, University of Oklahoma Press, 1934.

Loughlin, Patricia , *Hidden Treasures of the American West: Muriel H. Wright, Angie Debo, and Alice Marriott,* University of New Mexico Press, Albquerque, 2005.

Thoburn, Joseph and Muriel H. Wright, *Oklahoma: A History of the State and Its People,* 4 volumes, Lewis Historical Publishing Co. 1929.

Wright, Muriel, *Our Oklahoma,* Co-operative Publishing Co., Guthrie OK, 1930.

Fischer, LeRoy, "Muriel H. Wright, Historian of Oklahoma," *The Chronicles of Oklahoma* 52, Oklahoma City, OK., Spring 1974

Muriel Wright, Western History Collection, University of Oklahoma, Norman, Ok.

Muriel Wright, Vertical File, Oklahoma Department of Libraries, Oklahoma City, OK

Selected articles from the Daily Oklahoman from the Vertical File, ODL, OKC

Muriel Wright *Contemporary authors*,

Muriel Wright, Gale Literary Database,

Nomination form for Oklahoma Women's Hall of Fame, Governor's Advisory Committee on the Status of Women.

MABEL BASSETT

Moore, Jessie Randolph, "Tribute to Mabel Bassett," *The Chronicles of Oklahoma,*

Oklahoma City, OK. Winter,1954.

Hand, Elsie, "Mabel Bourne Bassett," *The Chronicles of Oklahoma*, Oklahoma City, OK, Winter, 1954.

Wright, Muriel, "Oklahoma Memorial Association Hall of Fame," *The Chronicles of Oklahoma,* Oklahoma City, OK, Winter, 1945.

Mabel Basssett, Vertical File, Oklahoma Department of Libraries, Oklahoma City, OK

Selected articles from the Daily Oklahoman from the Vertical File, ODL, OKC